谨以此书献给为新中国屯垦戍边作出贡献的人们

This book is dedicated to those who contributed to the military farming and border guarding for P.R.C.

英汉对照
Chinese-English

胡杨百咏

ODES TO DIVERSIFOLIOUS POPLARS

王瀚林◎著　杨虚◎译

By Wang Hanlin
Tr. Yang Xu

東方出版社

作者简介

　　王瀚林（1959.10—　），湖北天门人，文学学士，法学硕士，硕士研究生导师，现任新疆生产建设兵团党委宣传部副部长，中华诗词学会常务理事，兵团诗词楹联家协会主席。长期从事理论研究，主持国家课题《屯垦戍边理论研究》、《新兴媒体与边疆稳定发展》，协助课题组长并主笔完成《兵团精神研究》、《毛泽东屯垦思想研究》等国家课题。在各类刊物发表理论文章数十篇，代表作有《试论毛泽东屯垦思想》、《邓小平对毛泽东屯垦思想的重大贡献》、《论"三个代表"重要思想的理论创新》、《党中央重大战略思想对社会主义理论的丰富和创新》、《新疆生产建设兵团三十年改革实践的重大启示》、《在屯垦戍边新实践中体现共产党员的先进性》等。任总撰稿的专题片《千古之策》获电视金鹰奖。出版长篇史诗《屯垦戍边唱大风》、《中国历代屯垦戍边诗词选注》（合作）。主编出版《中国历代屯垦资料选注》、《辉煌与探索》、《迈向新世纪的屯垦事业》、《毛泽东屯垦思想与西部大开发》、《亲历激情岁月》（1—5卷）、《毛泽东屯垦思想研究论文选》、《践行"三个代表"，推进屯垦戍边》等著作。

| About the Author |

Wang Hanlin (Oct., 1959—), a native of Tianmen, Hubei Province, China, bachelor of art, master of law, and MA supervisor, is now vice director of the Publicity Department of the Party Committee of Xinjiang Production and Construction Corps, a standing council member of Chinese Poetry Society and president of Chinese Poetry and Couplet Association of the Corps. He is the author of the long epic *Border Guards' Songs on Military Farming*, and *Selection and Annotation of the Chinese Poems on Military Farming and Border Guarding Throughout the Ages* (in collaboration with others). He has been a theoretical researcher and is in charge of the national projects of "A Theoretical Study of Military Farming and Border Guarding" and "New Media and the Stability and Development of the Border Regions". He aided the group leader and was the main author of the research results of the following national projects: "A Study of the Corps' Spirit" and "A Study of Mao Zedong's Thought on Military Farming ". He has published dozens of theoretical articles on different journals and his representative works are: "On Mao Zedong's Thought on Military Farming", "Deng Xiaoping's Great Contribution to Mao Zedong's Thought on Military Farming", "On the Theoretical Creation of the Important Thought of 'Three Represents'", "The Enriching and Creation of the Party Central Committee's Important Strategical Thoughts to the Theory of Socialism", "The Great Revelation of the 30 Years of Reforming Practice of Xinjiang Production and Construction Corps" and "The Embodiment of Advancedness of the Communist Party Members in the New Practice of Military Farming and Border Guarding". The TV Special "The Time Tested Strategy" chiefly written by him won the Golden Eagle Award. He is also the compiler of *Selection and Annotation of the Materials on Military Farming Throughout the Ages in China, Glory and Exploration, The Cause of Military Farming towards the New Century, Mao Zedong's Thought on Military Farming and the Great Development of the West, Experiencing the Passionate Years* (Vols.1-5), *Selected Papers on the Study of Mao Zedong's Thought on Military Farming*, and *Practicing the Thought of "Three Represents" and Promoting Military Farming and Border Guarding.*

译者简介

杨虚（1962— ），字成虎，安徽舒城人。中国当代著名学者、诗人、翻译家。博士、教授、硕士生导师。1983 年本科毕业于安徽大学；1988 年研究生毕业于合肥工业大学；2008 年博士生毕业于北京师范大学。现在宁波大学工作，从事语言学、翻译学研究以及诗歌翻译工作。在各级学术刊物上发表论文 30 余篇；著有《复指与语法化问题研究》、《语言学普通读本》（合著）、《英美文学选读》、《现代英语语法》、《英语词汇学》、《竹云轩诗稿》、《楚辞传播学与英语语境问题研究》（合著）、《语法转喻的认知研究》、《中国诗歌典籍英译散论》等，译有《唐诗三百首》（合译）、《臧克家短诗选》、《李小雨短诗选》、《王学忠诗稿》、《心笛》（蔡丽双原著）、《人和蟒恋》（周毓明原著）、《纵横千山》（陈旭原著）、《20 世纪中国新诗选》（合译）、《3650 行阳光》（杨矿原著）、《太阳来的十秒钟》（合译）等。

| About the Translator |

Yang Xu (1962—), alias Chenghu, a native of Shucheng County, Anhui Province, China, is a famous scholar, poet and translator. He is now a Ph.D., professor of English and MA supervisor. He graduated from Anhui University in 1983 as an undergraduate, from Hefei Polytechnic University in 1988 as a postgraduate and in 2008 as a doctor from Beijing Normal University. Now, he works at Ningbo University. He is engaged in the study of Linguistics and Translatology as well as verse translation. He has published more than 30 papers in various journals. He is the author of *Epanalepses in Grammaticalization, A Primer in Linguistics* (in collaboration with others), *Selected Readings of British and American Literature, Modern English Grammar, English Lexicology, Poems of Bamboo-Cloud Study, A Cognitive Study of Metonymy in Grammar, Aspects of the English Translation of Chinese Verse Canons*, etc. He is the translator of *300 Tang Poems* (in collaboration with others), *Selected Short Poems of Zang Kejia, Selected Short Poems of Li Xiaoyu, Selected Poems of Wang Xuezhong, Heart-Flute* (the original by Choi Laisheung), *Love Between a Human Being and a Serpentine Being* (the original by Zhou Yuming), *Across Mountains* (the original by Chen Xu), *Selected New Chinese Poems of 20th Century* (in collaboration with others), *3650 Lines of Sunlight* (the original by Yang Kuang), *Ten Seconds from the Sun* (in collaboration with others), etc.

目 录

胡杨百咏

|Contents |

Odes to Diversifolious Poplars

序 李文朝

  这是一部由长期屯垦戍边的诗人创作推出的汉英对照本《胡杨百咏》七绝系列组诗。这组咏物诗以物喻人，借景抒情，抒发了当代边关将士和屯垦戍边官兵扎根边陲建设和保卫祖国的豪情壮志，是当代戍边人崇高精神的写照。

  胡杨是一种名垂千秋的树。它生而不死一千年，死而不倒一千年，倒而不朽一千年。我们赞美胡杨，是因为胡杨象征着为国戍边的革命军人和屯垦官兵；我们赞美胡杨精神，是因为胡杨的坚韧、执着、奉献精神与为了国家和人民利益，不怕艰难困苦，不怕流血牺牲，坚韧不拔，勇往直前的边关军魂具有天人合一的高度统一。

  胡杨是一种意志坚韧的树。恶劣的环境铸就了胡杨的钢筋铁骨，它不怕盐碱浸入骨髓，不惧风沙铺天盖地，即使在戈壁荒漠，它也照样枝繁叶茂，被誉为"沙漠的脊梁"，它的坚韧、挺拔和顽强，正像我们的战士，他们都用自己不屈不挠、不言放弃的精神书写着不朽的生命之歌。

  胡杨是一种雄奇壮美的树。幼苗时期枝条纤细而柔顺，婀娜妩媚；再稍大点，其叶细长青绿，生机盎然；再大些，胡杨换上一身抵御西北漠风的金甲，彰显沙漠之魂的刚毅和洒脱。胡杨之美与军人之美，都美在他们既伟岸威武，又饱含深情。

胡杨是一种甘于奉献的树。在沙漠死一般的沉寂中，它用春天的翠绿和秋天的金黄迎接年年岁岁的枯荣，固守着千年不变的信念。胡杨向人类索取很少，奉献很多，只需要几滴雨露一片阳光它就生长灿烂。除了生态价值和观赏价值之外，胡杨泪，流出的是制碱原料；胡杨根收藏的是根雕艺术。而且胡杨能够随遇而安，它絮状的种子随风飘散各地，遇土生根、见水发芽，这与我们的战士"哪里需要到哪里去，哪里艰苦哪里安家"有着共同的生存理念和精神境界。

胡杨又是一种根须深长的树。其根系深扎于几十米的地下，从地层深处吸取和输送水分，保证其生命常绿。它的根部细胞不会受到碱水的伤害，反而因其浓度较高而从富含盐碱的水中吸收水分和养料。坚强而生生不息的根，让胡杨以高傲的姿态向着高处生长。哪怕是沧海变成桑田，桑田变成沙漠，这伟大的根系依然支撑着胡杨千年不死。这一点也正是人民军队的精神写照，我们的军队也正是从人民群众中汲取无穷的力量，所以能够从小到大，战无不胜。

胡杨无语，但精神感人；胡杨无语，但风情诱人！多少人不远万里，扛着"长枪短炮"，来到胡杨伟岸的身旁，守候每个黎明日出和晚霞夕照，徜徉胡杨林中，拍不尽的画面，道不尽的思念，割不断的爱恋。你若懂胡杨，你一定会爱胡杨。

《胡杨百咏》让人们从胡杨看到了戍边人的价值与追求，看到了军人的伟大与崇高。在这个改革开放、开拓创新的伟大时代，弘扬这种精神意义重大而深远。

作者王瀚林先生是新疆生产建设兵团宣传部的领导，也是中华诗词学会常务理事。他的这 109 首七绝显示了他深厚的古体诗创作功底和古典诗歌修养。他古为今用，自觉继承了古典诗歌的传统，又深刻表现了当今时代的新意。这组诗在艺术想象上的开阔雄浑，意象创造上的奇异新颖以及对古代边塞诗的积极继承都给人以深刻的印象。

在开阔雄浑的艺术想象上，瀚林通过对胡杨树的描写，开拓了当代边疆"大漠孤烟直，长河落日圆"的新意境，这样的诗句有："漫卷高枝蘸晚霞，凌空巨笔画桑麻"（咏胡杨之一），"借得长风三万里，化成屯垦戍边郎"（咏胡杨之四十二），"万里边关万里金，扎根荒漠百年身"（咏胡杨之十），"莫道狂沙似海深，根深百尺有芳春"（咏胡杨之五十三），"铮铮铁骨弄风华，宛若苍龙戏晚霞"（咏胡杨之六十），"根盘百尺边陲固，一样龙沙别样天"（咏胡杨十九），"劫尽精华筋骨在，高枝剑指九重天"（咏胡杨之二十八）等。

在奇异新颖的意象创造上，瀚林将胡杨的形象与军人的精神予以巧妙的结合，写出了一些意象十分新颖的诗句，如："龙沙处处遗忠骨"（咏胡杨之二十九），将胡杨树的枯干喻作牺牲将士的忠骨，非常恰当，令人肃然起敬；"摧骨狂沙权当浴"（咏胡杨之七十），将四围卷起的沙尘暴喻作洗浴，宣示了军人们以苦为乐的情怀；"分明电闪时空退，疑是沙驼负重归"（咏胡杨之八十一），将处于雷鸣电闪乱光闪烁中的一行行胡杨树想象成负载而归的驼队，化静为动，又蕴含了它默默无闻甘于奉献的精神。

在继承边塞诗创作传统上，瀚林化用了许多中国诗歌史上的名句，如"狂飙漫卷龙沙起，送我诗情到碧霄"（咏胡杨之五）；"枯卧荒原不自悲，长思奋力洒芳菲"（咏胡杨之六十二），"此身不叹沧州老，长戍天山乐五更"（咏胡杨之一〇八），"荒原一望客心惊，满眼嶙嶙墓志铭"（咏胡杨之三十三）；"不知满眼杨花舞，疑是初冬雪满天"（咏胡杨之八十七）等，都能读出古代边塞诗句的韵味。这些诗句的化用说明诗作者不但在精神上继承了边塞诗的思想，而且在语言层面也能将前人的诗句灵活运用。

据翻译家们介绍，作为汉英对照的一部诗集，这组七绝的英译文也能够体现原作的风貌。译者在多年翻译和创作经验的基础上，使用了相应的诗体，注意了语言的韵律性和转译的传神性，必要的地方采用了注释。译文采用第二人称以对话的方式将"咏胡杨"表现为对胡杨的直接称颂，诗句十分流畅，读来亲切。相信通过英文译本的传播，胡杨精神和中国戍边人的风采，能够得到更广泛的宣扬。

由于我曾是中央电视台军事节目中心主任，在工作岗位上时多次带领摄制组到新疆包括生产建设兵团及其他边防部队采访，退下来后又到中华诗词学会工作。瀚林先生正是抓住了我的军旅和诗词双重情结，执意让我写序，再三推辞不过，只好从命为之。是为序。

2013 年 7 月 15 日于北京

| Preface |

Li Wenchao

At my hand is a set of Chinese-English seven-character quatrains called *Odes to the Diversifolious Poplars* composed by a soldier-poet who has long been serving in Xinjiang, China. This set of lyrical odes compares diversifolious poplars to soldiers as a noble expression of the army men safeguarding and farming at the frontier. It is a reflection of the lofty spirit of our contemporary border guards.

Diversifolious poplars are trees of endurance. They live for a thousand years, stand for a thousand years after death and keep their remnants for a thousand years though fallen. We eulogize them as they stand for our frontiersmen and farming army men; we eulogize their spirit of steadfast devotion as it merges with the army spirit of braving hardships and bloodshed.

Diversifolious poplars are trees of strong willpower. They are tempered in unfavorable conditions, never afraid of the penetrating alkali or avalanches of sandstorms. They are luxuriant even in Gobi deserts and are named "the backbones in the sands". Like our soldiers, their firmness, loftiness, stubbornness and determination are just a song of everlasting life.

Diversifolious poplars are trees of great beauty. They are slender and tender in their infancy, brow-leafed and vigorous in their childhood and sturdy and graceful in their adulthood when they are gold-armored in the sands. They resemble our army men in that they are lofty, valiant and affectionate.

Diversifolious poplars are trees of dedication. With their eternal faith, they greet the passage of time with their verdant color in spring and golden hue in autumn. They take little from but give much to humans. They live a brilliant life only with a few dewdrops and some rays of sunlight. Besides their ecological and aesthetical worth, they give off a sap which is the raw material for alkali and offer their roots for sculpture. They sprout and take roots wherever their downy seeds go. And such a spirit is shared by our soldiers who "settle wherever they are needed."

Diversifolious poplars are trees of deep roots as well. They take roots as deep as dozens of meters underground absorbing and transfusing water for their life. The cells of their roots are immune to the alkali. Rather, they take water and nutrients from the highly concentrated solution of salt and alkali. The great intricacy of the firm and enlivening roots enable them to grow skyward and live for a thousand years in the vicissitudes of the world, which, too, is a spiritual reflection of the people's army. Our army, in the same way, takes its great vitality from among the people in its robust growth.

Diversifolious poplars are movingly and attractively taciturn. Many people come to them from afar with cameras, greeting every sunrise and sunset here. In such forest, they enjoy their scenes, appreciate their beauties and extend to them their loving concerns. You must have fallen in love with them if you understand them.

Odes to Diversifolious Poplars enables us to see the worth and pursuit of our border guards, the greatness and nobility of our soldiers. It is of far-reaching significance to give a full expression to such a spirit in our era of reformation, creation and opening to the outside world.

Mr. Wang Hanlin, the author of this set of quatrains, is a member of the leadership of the Publicity Department of Xinjiang Production and Construction Corps and the standing council member of Chinese Poetry Society as well. His 109 quatrains is an expression of the profundity of his poetic creation of classical styles of Chinese poetry and his accomplishment of traditional Chinese poetry. He made use of such a tradition in the contemporary time and theme. This set of quatrains is imposing in that it is grand, magnificent and novel in the creation of images and that it is an active continuation of the border poetry in the ancient times.

In the grand creation of images, the author has opened up a new realm of the contemporary scenes at the frontier. Examples are: "Your branches tower into clouds in twilight/Which serve to paint a good farmland in sight"(No.1); "You came all the way to light in this place,/As a farming soldier, crops you have grown"(No.42); "A thousand miles of passes as well as gold/Is the place you live all your life and hold"(No.10); "Never say that ocean-like is th' wild sand /In which your long roots preserve vernal strand"(No.53); "Your iron of bones displays your look proud,/As if you're a dragon in th' rosy cloud"(No.60); "Deeply rooted in th' uppermost frontier,/You make a different world in th' sands vast"(No.19); "Your bones remain though you died in kalpas,/With your skyward bough like a fighting hand"(No.28), etc.

In the creation of novel images, Hanlin has artistically combined the image of the diversifolious poplar and the spirit of the contemporary soldiers, having produced such fresh lines as: "Your loyal bones left everywhere in sands"(No.29), appropriately comparing the trees' dried trunks to the bones of the dead soldiers, creating a result of respect; "The bone-breaking storm is just bath for you"(No.70), comparing the sandstorm in the sands to a bath for soldiers, airing the soldiers' pleasure in hardships; "You're camel teams on your way back with loads / When lightning and thunder go back to th' sky"(No.81), imagining rows of diversifolious poplars in thunder and lightning into camel teams with loads, turning the static into motion, and in the meantime, creating the soldiers' spirit of dedication and devotion in obscurity.

Hanlin has inherited much of the tradition of the classical Chinese Poetry in a wealth of quatrains. For example, "While th' golden tide of golden boughs and leaves, /Makes my sky-reaching poetic heart proud"(No.5); "O'er the barren land never feeling sad, /You endeavor to spread the green you've had"(No.62); "You ne'er regret getting old in Cangzhou, /You e'en enjoy safeguarding Tianshan, though."(No.108); "A look at the wasteland will one surprise, / Rows of your stone inscriptions meet his eyes."(No.33); "Not knowing catkins dancing before eyes, / They can be snowflakes on the winter's ride"(No.87), etc. Such lines carry the sources from classical poetry. The author's uses of these sources show that he has not only inherited the spirit of the classical poetry on borders and frontiers, but also follows some patterns of lines in terms of words and images.

I am told by the translators round me that as a bilingual version, the English version of this set of quatrains are faithful to the original Chinese in terms of style. On the basis of his years of translating and creating experiences, the translator has applied corresponding forms with enough attention paid to the metrics and poetics. In addition, he has made use of necessary notes. He uses the second person and the style of dialogues to eulogize diversifolious poplars in terms of odes. The translated lines make a fluent and endearing reading. I'm sure that the spirituality of diversifolious poplars and the style of the Chinese border guards will get more widely known through the translator's effort.

I was the director of the center of military programs of CCTV, and had interviews with the border troops including Xinjiang Production and Construction Corps when I led the photographic group to Xinjiang, and after I retired, I have been working at Chinese Poetry Society. Hanlin insists that he invite me to write a preface to his work as affectionately I have been both a soldier and a poet. I can in no way turn down his invitation. Hence this preface.

Beijing   July 15, 2013

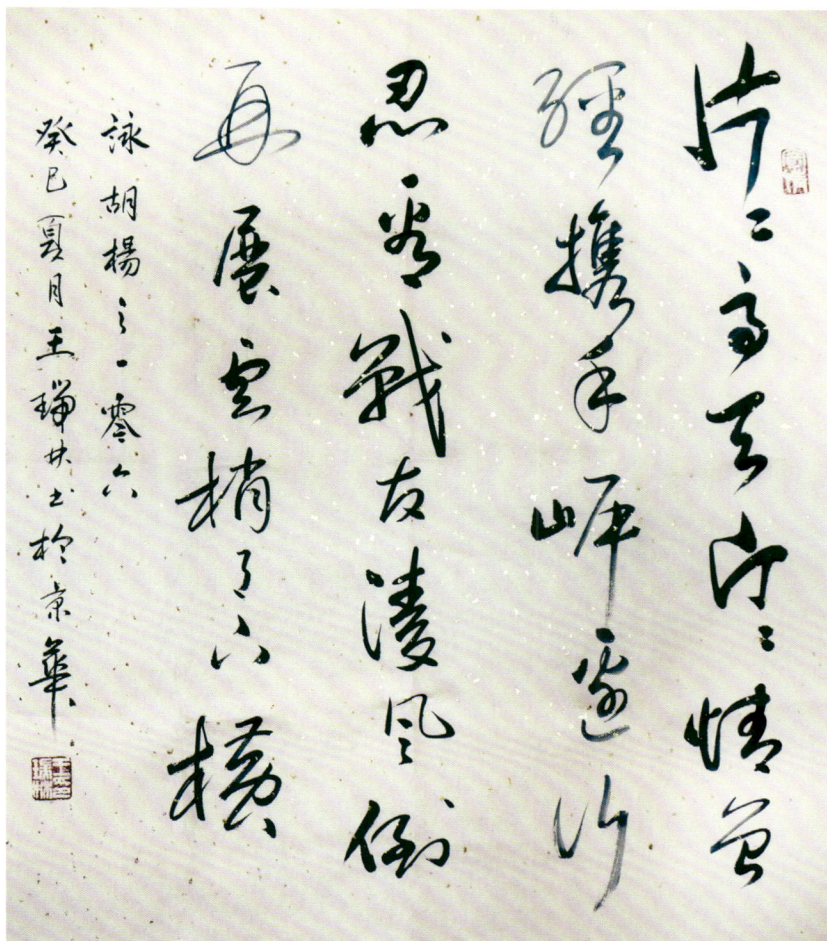

片片真心吐情愫
轻携手姊妹情
忍霜战友凌风俏
更堪擎天六横

咏胡杨二〇一六
癸巳夏月王瑞林书于京华

王瑞林

中国著名书画家，中国书画艺术研究院副院长。

高　峰

中国书法家协会会员，著名书法家。

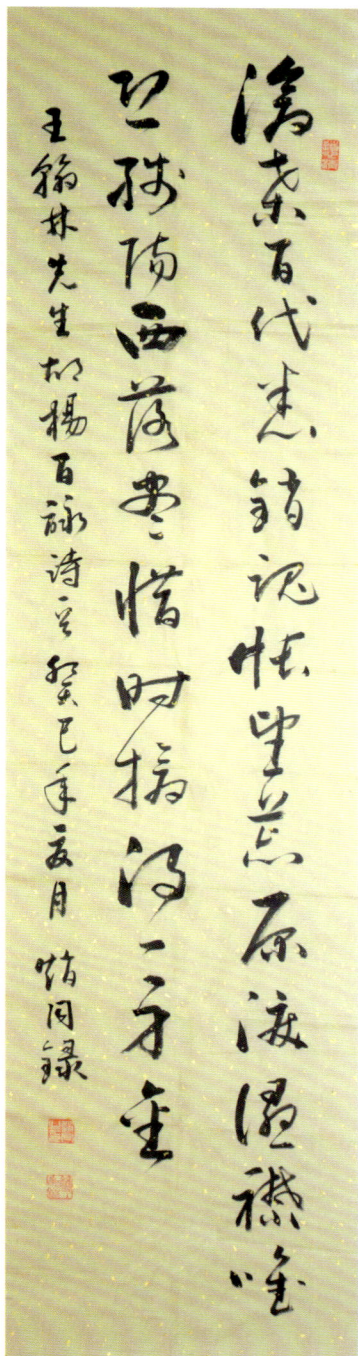

潇洒百代走，销魂帖里藏。原液温禄鑫，卫殊陶西落，情时搞冯三才垒

王翁林先生胡杨百咏诗一章　癸巳年孟月　怡同录

赵　同

中国书法家协会会员，著名书法家。

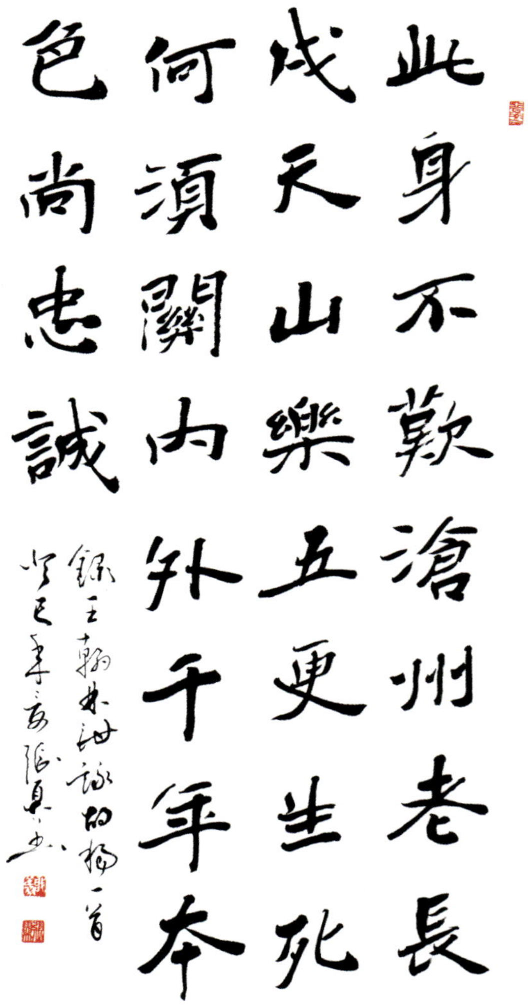

此身不歎滄州老長

戍天山樂五更生死

何須關內外千年本

色尚忠誠

錄王翰朱地球的楊一首

雲主書 張冀 書

张 冀
中国美术家联谊会会员、中国书法国画研究院会员。
1993 年荣获"我们盼奥运"五环旗书法竞赛毛笔书法一等奖。

沈　鹏

中央直属机关书画协会理事、北京师白艺术研究会副秘书长、
中国人民大学沈鹏艺术馆副馆长、沈鹏书法艺术学校名誉副校长。

何耀军

北京皇家园林书画研究会理事、中艺卿云书画院常务理事。

窦火胡杨撲面
来苍颜未老叶
先衰多情我歎
长相守化作芦
苍脚下开

翰林先生胡杨诗一首 李仁

岁在癸巳

李 仁
中国书画家，北京书画艺术研究会会员。

田晓刚

号田夫，被文化部授予"世界华人艺术家"、
"世界书画艺术名人"荣誉称号。

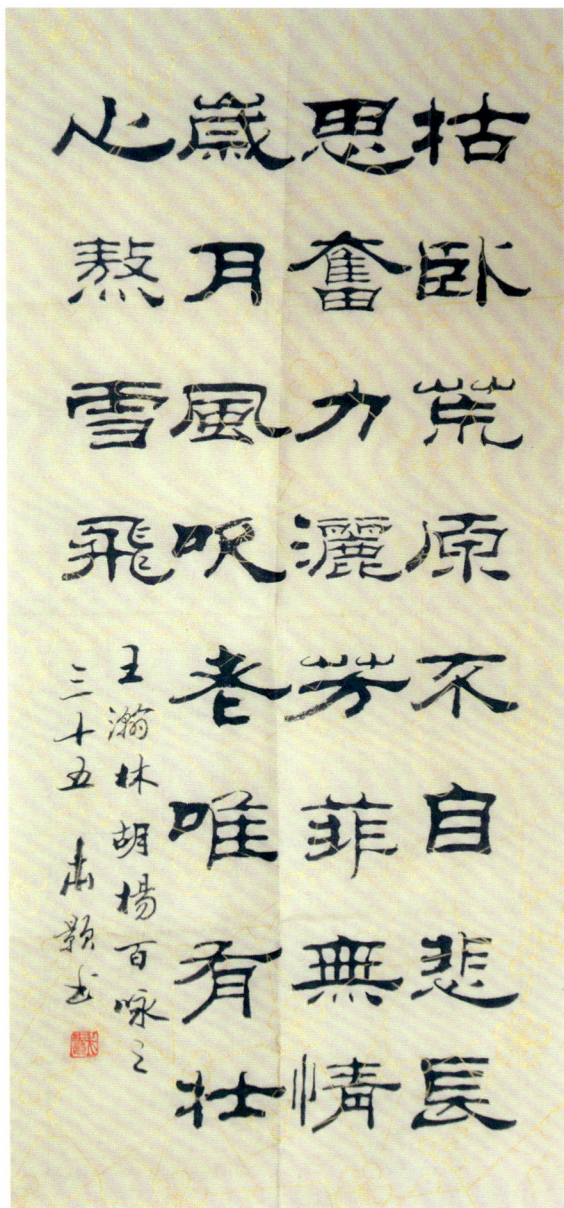

戴本颢

中国书法家，新疆书画学会副会长。

云乃楷诗日色涂金枝举

萦赋金梁往飘漫搀龙沙

趋迤秉诗情新碧霄

王瀚林先生咏胡杨诗之四甲午二月梁文源书

梁文源

新疆书法家协会常务理事。

漫卷高枝醒晚霞浓
其巨笔画意庶绘成
方外清之胃南唯尼水
疑是咏

录王瀚校先生胡杨百咏
甲午夏作澄画之

章海安
中国书画家协会会员，楷书委员会委员。

咏胡杨

之一

漫卷高枝蘸晚霞，
凌空巨笔画桑麻。
绘成方外清清界，
南雁飞来疑是家。

Odes to Diversifolious Poplars (No.1)

Your branches tower into clouds in twilight
Which serve to paint a good farmland in sight—
A view of peacefulness beyond the world
Where southern swans will fly over and light.

咏胡杨

之二

沧桑百代悉销魂，

怅望荒原泪湿襟。

唯恐残阳西落尽，

惜时抢得一身金。

Odes to Diversifolious Poplars (No.2)

Saddening all changing ages in th' past,
Tears wet your wear with a distant look cast;
The remaining sun setting down the wasteland,
You seize the chance to own its gold-rays last.

咏胡杨

之三

冰霜雨雪久为邻，
绿遍荒原金满屯。
有意置身风景外，
谁知已是画中人。

Odes to Diversifolious Poplars (No.3)

You've long accompanied with frost and ice,
Greening th' whole wasteland with gold in great size;
Already a figure in the fine view,
You try to prevent yourself from our eyes.

咏胡杨

之四

鸿雁南翔何日归，

忍看槁叶接天飞。

归来借得银河水，

水沃荒滩春色肥。

Odes to Diversifolious Poplars (No.4)

When to return the south-flying wild swan
Seeing the dead leaves roam about like bran.
It may bring the celestial water here
To offer the wasteland a vernal plan.

咏胡杨

之五

云过梢头日色消，
金枝金叶赋金潮。
狂飙漫卷龙沙起，
送我诗情到碧霄。

Odes to Diversifolious Poplars (No.5)

Darkening the sun is the o'er-tree cloud,
Where the desert is whirled up by gales loud,
While th' golden tide of golden boughs and leaves,
Makes my sky-reaching poetic heart proud.

咏胡杨

之六

云锦胡桐叶带丝，
低头不是弄风姿。
未施粉黛犹惊世，
尽道君妆最入时。

Odes to Diversifolious Poplars (No.6)

The brocade of your needle-leaves is fine,
Bowing your head which is not a coy sign.
Shocking the world without any makeup,
Your appearance is among the best line.

咏胡杨

之七

满目黄金犯碛开，

高枝疏处白云来。

羌笛一曲胡天静，

孤雁闻声曾不哀。

Odes to Diversifolious Poplars (No.7)

Your golden boughs brighten the great sand,
Over which white clouds gather and expand.
A play of the western flute is heard here,
Gladdening the wild swans over this land.

咏胡杨

之八

陌上遥观风雪姿，

冰心傲骨赋清词。

茫茫草叶归沉寂，

蓦见君将军礼持。

Odes to Diversifolious Poplars (No.8)

Behold! You stand like a soldier upright
There on the way in wind strong and snow white,
When the far-stretching grass into silence falls,
But with a lofty mind you seem to write.

咏胡杨

之九

芳心到死不轻抒，

针叶绵绵近似无。

直到黄金铺满地，

时人方悟四时殊。

Odes to Diversifolious Poplars (No.9)

Your needle-leaves too small and fine to be seen,
Your steadfast heart has always so pure been.
People begin to know you are special
Until you've created a golden scene.

咏胡杨

之十

万里边关万里金，
扎根荒漠百年身。
由他沙卷西风烈，
苦难辉煌铸我魂。

Odes to Diversifolious Poplars (No.10)

A thousand miles of passes as well as gold
Is the place you live all your life and hold.
In devastating sandstorms and west wind,
The hardship and glory make your soul bold.

咏胡杨

之十一

落尽群芳君立时，
黄金万两在繁枝。
有人来借全拿去，
借据一抛风上吹。

Odes to Diversifolious Poplars (No.11)

You still stand high there while other flowers fall,
Your boughs are laden with gold best of all.
The receipt is thrown and blown in the wind
When someone need this gold to whate'er call.

咏胡杨

之十二

爱君如画又如歌，
叶盖浓云影半遮。
莫向人间展金色，
贪家掠去竞豪奢。

Odes to Diversifolious Poplars (No.12)

You are a lovely picture or a song,
Your leaves covering clouds and shades in throng.
Ne'er show your golden hue to th' human world,
In case that th' greedy make it suffer wrong.

咏胡杨

之十三

过水穿林草木零，
遥闻有女踏歌声。
眼前疑似金龙阵，
身在当年细柳营。

Odes to Diversifolious Poplars (No.13)

Through rivers and forests where weeds are drear,
Songs sung by a girl are heard far and near.
It seems a gold dragon array before eyes,
And you in th' Willow Camp in an old year.

咏胡杨

之十四

秋来塞外晚风香，
玉女罗裙绿上黄。
相映红颜如一洗，
为她灿烂似朝阳。

Odes to Diversifolious Poplars (No.14)

Fragrant breezes waft west here in the fall,
Where the ladies' skirts are the hues of all.
That join in the green to make a new view,
A view so sunny in the forest tall.

咏胡杨

之十五

穿林旭日照清泉，

红袖凭栏对影看。

道是水中人物好，

不知借水已登天。

Odes to Diversifolious Poplars (No.15)

Shining o'er brooks the sunbeams through woods go,
Whose scene to a lady does itself show.
She praises the figures as mirrored there,
Not knowing they ascend the sky in the flow.

咏胡杨

之十六

轻风抚面对妆台，

含笑君从镜底来。

十里金黄何所似？

任人想象任人猜。

Odes to Diversifolious Poplars (No.16)

At the dressing table breeze strokes your face,
You come from the mirror with smiling grace.
What does it look like, the ten miles of gold?
In imagination, th' scene one can trace.

咏胡杨

之十七

云来雁去北风号，

奈我春心下碧霄。

瀚海冬装裹不住，

老根暗发几株苗。

Odes to Diversifolious Poplars (No.17)

In all weather of cloud and wind and rain
My heart will descend from the azure main
And some new sprouts appear on old roots
Which the vast wintry desert can't refrain.

咏胡杨

之十八

树前久立问青天，

何为经霜未老颜？

蔽日繁枝沙漠里，

盘根已到塔河边。

Odes to Diversifolious Poplars (No.18)

I ask Heaven standing before the tree
Why you keep yourself as young as can be
With your roots extending far and wide
Shading the desert with your leaves in glee.

Note: In the translation of the last line, a special geographical name River
Ta is omitted for the convenience of meter. Instead, "far and wide" is used.

咏胡杨

之十九

历夏经冬挺益坚，

凌风抗旱我当先。

根盘百尺边陲固，

一样龙沙别样天。

Odes to Diversifolious Poplars (No.19)

Throughout the seasons you stand e'er steadfast,
Against droughts to be a van-guard you asked.
Deeply rooted in th' uppermost frontier,
You make a different world in th' sands vast.

咏胡杨

之二十

沧桑阅尽爱心存，
瀚海扎根百尺深。
生来就是恋荒漠，
婚外无情直到今。

Odes to Diversifolious Poplars (No.20)

The world had changed but your love remain,
With your roots planted deep in the sand's main.
You are born to love the great desert here,
So faithful that you have no other brain.

咏胡杨

之二十一

盘根千载意何求？

唯愿边畴尽绿洲。

岂与群芳争俏丽，

寸心热血写风流。

Odes to Diversifolious Poplars (No.21)

Your aim of age-old intricate roots' net
Is to make oases in the border set
Rather than vie beauty with other flowers
So that special grace you strive for and get.

咏胡杨
之二十二

冬去春来应换装，
小花脱尽叶初黄。
休言此处风沙苦，
逢必与人称故乡。

Odes to Diversifolious Poplars (No.22)

You change your dresses from winter to spring,
And after catkins yellow sprouts you bring.
Mentioning no hardship of sandstorms here,
To others of your living place you sing.

咏胡杨

之二十三

搏击风沙百战身，

纵难取义也成仁。

千年不倒真魂在，

大象仍留吓鬼神。

Odes to Diversifolious Poplars (No.23)

You have fought many battles of sandstorm,
Justice and benevolence as your norm.
Your spirit remains where your trunk stands tall,
Scaring away demons with your great form.

咏胡杨

之二十四

日落黄尘远接天，
龙盘虎踞夜无眠。
残躯虽老神威在，
一觑豺狼尽胆寒。

Odes to Diversifolious Poplars (No.24)

The yellow dusts reach the sky at sunset,
And there paramount yourself you have set.
Old as you are, so valiant you remain,
Which to avaricious wolves is a threat.

咏胡杨

之二十五

一道风鞭一道痕，
群芳谢后见精神。
姑娘笑我苍颜老，
我有天心不染尘。

Odes to Diversifolious Poplars (No.25)

A bruise after a whip of the strong gale,
Your spirit is seen when other flowers fail.
Gentile young ladies mock at your old age
While your natural power will never go pale.

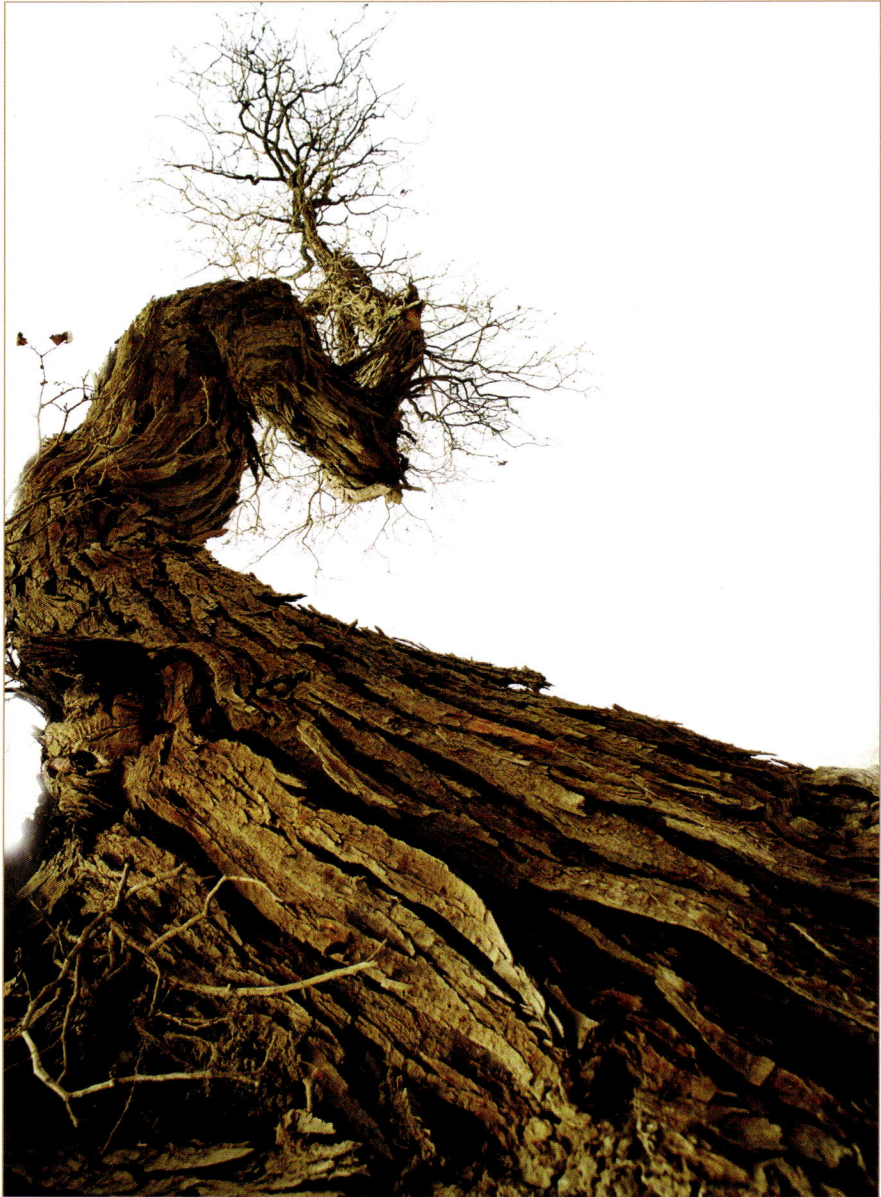

咏胡杨

之二十六

百转虬龙覆大荒，
斑痕累累不言伤。
豪情未减难称老，
折臂君闻是否香？

Odes to Diversifolious Poplars (No.26)

You're a coiling dragon o'er the wasteland,
With bruises on your body you still stand.
You are never old with your passion strong,
Though broken, you still own a graceful hand.

咏胡杨

之二十七

老去犹能立大荒，
不知此地是他乡。
擎天一帜寒沙上，
还为游人作导航。

Odes to Diversifolious Poplars (No.27)

In your old age, in th' desert you still stand,
Not knowing that 'tis not your own homeland.
Serving as a guide for the travelers there,
You are just a banner o'er the cold sand.

咏胡杨

之二十八

黑沙尘骤起孤烟，
宛若苍龙舞破原。
劫尽精华筋骨在，
高枝剑指九重天。

Odes to Diversifolious Poplars (No.28)

A curl of smoke arises from dark sand,
Like wildly dancing dragon black and grand.
Your bones remain though you died in kalpas,
With your skyward bough like a fighting hand.

咏胡杨

之二十九

无定长河似转轮，
仪容数改为图存。
龙沙处处遗忠骨，
触目谁人不断魂。

Odes to Diversifolious Poplars (No.29)

Like a running wheel runs the Wuding Stream,
To change for survival its course does seem.
Your loyal bones left everywhere in sands,
Sadden people as with them th' place does teem.

咏胡杨

之三十

无语残骸动地哀，

伤心树下久徘徊。

不堪细读沧桑处，

似诉黄沙掣电来。

Odes to Diversifolious Poplars (No.30)

These silent and sad remnants shake the ground,

In sorrow I linger for long them round.

I fear to browse the bruises you endured,

Sandstorm with lightning joins your fighting sound.

咏胡杨

之三十一

独立沙丘护大荒，
如今皮破袒胸膛。
肚脐已做仙人洞，
且把沧桑拟断肠。

Odes to Diversifolious Poplars (No.31)

Standing alone to guard the great wasteland,
Now you have many a bruise and a brand.
Your navel has turned into a big cave,
Alas, a change of the world does expand.

咏胡杨

之三十二

龙沙盛夏起青烟，
中路驼铃响未还。
凝望枯枝疑是骨，
归来六月尚心寒。

Odes to Diversifolious Poplars (No.32)

In mid-summer, smoke arises from the sand,
Where faint are the bells of the camel band.
Your withered boughs seem to be your old bones,
Which freeze our heart e'en in the native land.

咏胡杨

之三十三

荒原一望客心惊，

满眼嶙嶙墓志铭。

移步近前观细节，

碱欧盐柳储真情。

注：欧指欧体，柳指柳体。此处形容盐碱存储在胡杨体内
留下的痕迹仿佛书法家的字迹。

Odes to Diversifolious Poplars (No.33)

A look at the wasteland will one surprise,
Rows of your stone inscriptions meet his eyes.
He comes to browse your stones in great detail,
To see your art of Ou and Liu styles arise.

Note: Ou refers to the Ouyang Xun's style of calligraphy and Liu to the Liu
Gongquan's style of calligraphy. Here, the calligraphic styles refer to the traces of
alkali and salt left in the diversifolious poplars which look like calligraphy.

咏胡杨

之三十四

荒郊独立晚云昏，
谁比晚云忧更勤。
干上沟渠谁凿出，
如麻雨脚印沙痕。

Odes to Diversifolious Poplars (No.34)

Standing alone there in the cloud of night,
An impending rain you are going to fight.
Who has cut the traces over your trunk?
The raindrops and sands making the sight.

咏胡杨

之三十五

一段枯根一段情，
余温犹在自销魂。
此生用尽绵绵力，
不计人前身后名。

Odes to Diversifolious Poplars (No.35)

A fraction of the dried root is a tale,
So moving that it makes one even wail.
You have given all your strength in your life,
Hiding your fame and deed without a trail.

咏胡杨

之三十六

老株折臂护新枝，

恰似欲燃正午时。

满眼葱茏都是爱，

此心鉴日几人知？

Odes to Diversifolious Poplars (No.36)

The broken old arm safeguards the new one,
Whose passion is like the burning noon sun.
All luxuriance' fore eyes is from your love,
Who knows your heart of brilliant piety? None!

咏胡杨

之三十七

尼雅楼兰何处寻?

胡桩未朽有遗箴。

毋需慧眼知材用,

自把荒沙百炼金。

Odes to Diversifolious Poplars (No.37)

Niya and Loulan, th' old lands where to find?
Th' poplar stumbles are lessons left behind.
No need to be known by anyone wise,
You know how to turn sand into th' best kind.

咏胡杨

之三十八

风刀乱剪冷参差，
一入黄沙志未移。
谁解君怀高远志，
时人尽向柳腰迷。

Odes to Diversifolious Poplars (No.38)

In the scissors of winds and depth of cold,
And in yellow sand, your willpower you hold.
Yet, who can understand your lofty goal,
See how many people are common-souled.

咏胡杨

之三十九

晚沙树影弄云深，
引得狂飙妒杀人。
寒叶风中散无数，
来年不变是春心。

Odes to Diversifolious Poplars (No.39)

You represent spring in the coming year,
In the cold showers of countless leaves so drear,
Where so jealous are strong and maddened gales,
And in dim shadows of sand you appear.

咏胡杨

之四十

舍命陪君融大荒，

好将热血化玄黄。

风沙敲梦披星起，

腹里豪情滚国殇。

Odes to Diversifolious Poplars (No.40)

With all efforts you root yourself in th' land

Of vast desert where your love does expand;

In storms of sand you rise from starlit dreams,

E'en if you fall, you keep your mission grand.

咏胡杨

之四十一

风骚独领三千载，
竭尽忠诚洗尽尘。
枝可崩摧头可断，
岿然不倒是精神。

Odes to Diversifolious Poplars (No.41)

Leading th' way for three thousand years in all,
With your devotion that no dust can sprawl;
Your branches and head may be cut away,
Yet your lofty spirit will never fall.

咏胡杨

之四十二

不知何处是家乡，
问祖寻根本姓杨。
借得长风三万里，
化成屯垦戍边郎。

Odes to Diversifolious Poplars (No.42)

Your native town has always been unknown,
But your ancestral name of Poplar's shown.
You came all the way to light in this place,
As a farming soldier, crops you have grown.

咏胡杨

之四十三

春生夏长到秋红，
景色四时难一同。
唯有平凡孕浩气，
始得寒岁显英雄。

Odes to Diversifolious Poplars (No.43)

Different scenes in four seasons appear,
With hues from sprouting to flourishing here.
The grandeur that grows in the test of time
Makes you a giant in the cold of the year.

咏胡杨

之四十四

古道凌风送驼影，
枕沙卧碱梦无声。
堪惊漠北多奇士，
恰似边城百万兵。

Odes to Diversifolious Poplars (No.44)

You see camels off along the old course,
You dream in the sands but never indoors.
Countless are your poses in the northwest,
An army of a million guarding force.

咏胡杨

之四十五

微风昨夜拍窗棂，

杨絮低飞入梦轻。

梦把银河无尽水，

换成荒漠树长青。

Odes to Diversifolious Poplars (No.45)

Breezes caressing the window last night,
Where enter my dream catkins in low flight.
Drawing the water from heavenly stream,
I want to evergreen these trees in sight.

咏胡杨

之四十六

御风抗碱固边防，
壮士脊梁护大荒。
堪笑江南湖畔柳，
余暇尽日逐春芳。

Odes to Diversifolious Poplars (No.46)

'Gainst wind and alkali at the frontier,
The grand land the heroes of these trees rear,
That mocks at the lakeside willows in the South
Which seek after the tenderness all the year.

咏胡杨

之四十七

多情看似恰无情，
深隐荒原情最深。
老去无名终不悔，
立身塞外舞清音。

Odes to Diversifolious Poplars (No.47)

Your deep emotion seems quite a stone-heart,
In th' desert you play a secluded part.
You ne'er regret getting old and obscure,
Living at th' frontier being your best art.

咏胡杨

之四十八

历尽沧桑何自怜，

冲天依旧气当年。

虬枝画满风沙色，

大限三千也等闲。

Odes to Diversifolious Poplars (No.48)

Proud of yourself throughout the changing world,
You pierce th' sky with your bravery unfurled.
Your intricate twigs stand high in sandstorms,
Even when th' living circumstances hurled.

咏胡杨

之四十九

掩泪行人戈壁游，
一看一叹一回头。
此身虽与沉沙没，
不废精神万古流。

Odes to Diversifolious Poplars (No.49)

Travelers return their heads and make sighs,
Seeing you herein with their tearful eyes.
Though in th' Gobi desert buried you are,
Your eternal spirit like rivers lies.

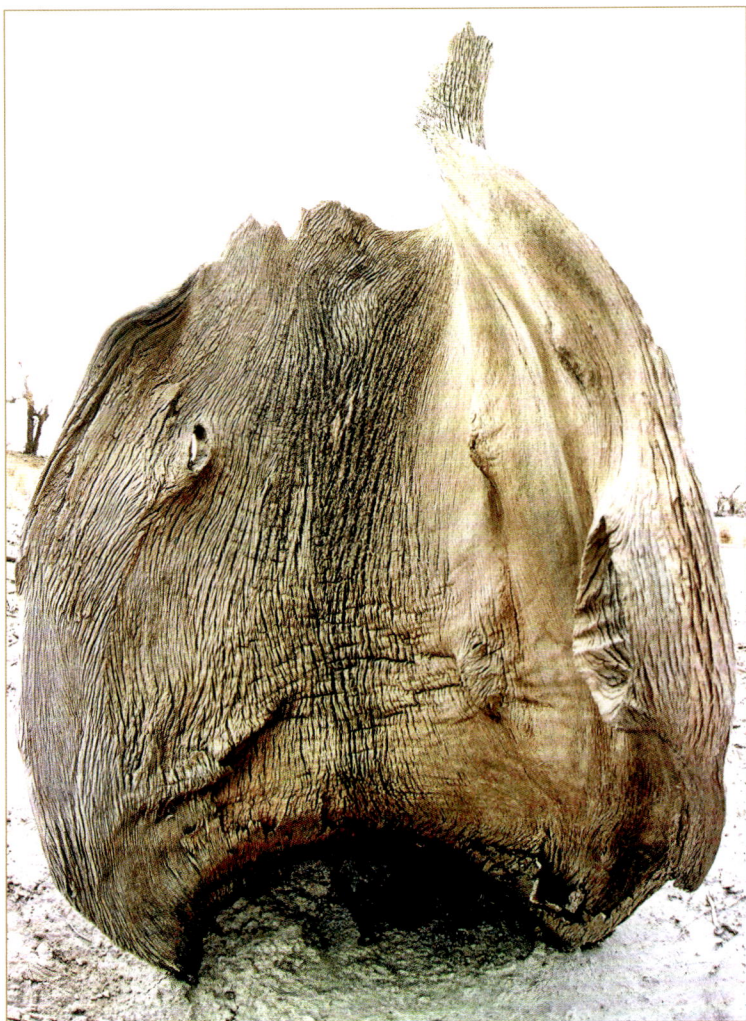

咏胡杨

之五十

一睹虬枝万种哀，
戎衣战尽剩残骸。
千年喋血何堪忆，
往事偏偏入梦来。

Odes to Diversifolious Poplars (No.50)

Your twisted boughs make a saddening sight,
Your bones remain though you're stripped in the fight.
A thousand years' bloodsheds, no way to tell,
But in dreams those bygones take their own right.

咏胡杨

之五十一

洪壑深埋劫后桠，
云峰极目是天涯。
何方借得愚公铲，
掘尽龙沙换绿芽。

Odes to Diversifolious Poplars (No.51)

Your boughs deeply buried in the ditch great,
To the high cloud you extend your eyes straight.
How can an earth-removing spade be found
To undo th' sands so that sprouts lie in wait.

咏胡杨

之五十二

惊沙乱海起风尘，
千古楼兰何处寻？
一自胡天有神木，
无边荒漠似还魂。

Odes to Diversifolious Poplars (No.52)

Nowhere found is Loulan the ancient land
In the vast ocean of the stormy sand;
The great desert has become a new world
Since the Northwest boasted its Poplars grand.

咏胡杨

之五十三

莫道狂沙似海深，

根深百尺有芳春。

问君生命何如此？

本是悬壶济世人。

Odes to Diversifolious Poplars (No.53)

Never say that ocean-like is th' wild sand
In which your long roots preserve vernal strand.
Why do you own vitality as such?
You are born to be a world-saving hand.

咏胡杨

之五十四

风里折枝如捋髯，
尚思奉碱遗人间。
古今多少弄娇木，
鉴此胡为不自惭。

Odes to Diversifolious Poplars (No.54)

You seem to just to stroke your beard in wind
With your offering alkaloid so kind.
Countless delicate plants throughout the times
Ashamed of their weakness themselves should find.

咏胡杨

之五十五

中年倍感日头长，
自有基因防晒伤。
若使春风能助我，
黄沙瘦土总无妨。

Odes to Diversifolious Poplars (No.55)

In your middle-age you feel the days long
With your special gene to prevent scorch strong.
If vernal breeze could offer you a hand,
Yellow sand and poor soil make nothing wrong.

咏胡杨

之五十六

时人皓首费思量，
不恋葱茏恋大荒。
日日留春春去也，
还舒老臂驻残阳。

Odes to Diversifolious Poplars (No.56)

The present people fail to understand why
You choose to love the desert and live by.
Failing to keep the spring which goes away,
You stretch your arms to stay the sun on high.

咏胡杨

之五十七

黄袍掩体似戎装，

不为封疆为戍疆。

誓与狂沙终日夜，

断肠新补旧衣裳。

Odes to Diversifolious Poplars (No.57)

Like an army robe is your yellow hue,
In place of profit, the frontier guard you.
You vow to stand in sandstorm day and night,
And with a broken heart your dress renew.

咏胡杨

之五十八

昨夜长风九万里，
是谁送我到边关？
沙中自有情和义，
好写人间大爱篇。

Odes to Diversifolious Poplars (No.58)

Who is it that sent you to the frontier
In last night's gale that traveled far off here?
Surely there's passion and justice in th' sands
Which will produce great love humans feel dear.

咏胡杨

之五十九

孤寂含情立漠原，
几经沧海志犹坚。
苦身播绿非吾乐，
只恐来生复涕涟。

Odes to Diversifolious Poplars (No.59)

You stand alone with passion in this land,
Remaining steadfast in changes so grand.
With hardship and pleasure you spread green shade,
But fear that your next life be drowned in sand.

咏胡杨

之六十

铮铮铁骨弄风华，
宛若苍龙戏晚霞。
瀚海男儿钟本性，
不求赘入五侯家。

Odes to Diversifolious Poplars (No.60)

Your iron of bones displays your look proud,
As if you're a dragon in th' rosy cloud.
Your lofty trunks boast of their own will
Which will never among tender flowers crowd.

咏胡杨

之六十一

狂飙卷地乱云飞，

驼刺梭梭伏地悲。

唯恐风中春去远，

朝朝啼血唤春归。

Odes to Diversifolious Poplars (No.61)

Wild clouds sweeping the skies and gales the ground
Where tears of Alhagi pseudalhagi are found
That fears the fast passage of vernal days
And cries its heart out to let spring come round.

Note: In the second line of the original Chinese verse, there is a kind of tree called sacsaoul (Holoxylon ammodendron) which is mentioned together with Alhagi pseudalhagi. Here the term is omitted as a result of the metric factor in the translated line.

咏胡杨

之六十二

枯卧荒原不自悲，
长思奋力洒芳菲。
无情岁月风吹老，
唯有壮心熬雪飞。

Odes to Diversifolious Poplars (No.62)

O'er the barren land never feeling sad,
You endeavor to spread the green you've had.
You have grown old all through the cruel years,
Howe'er, o'erwhelming the snow's your heart glad.

咏胡杨

之六十三

一树殷情一任天，
影形相伴立河沿。
尘沙携电飞来急，
前者横尸后展颜。

Odes to Diversifolious Poplars (No.63)

In all weathers you stand against the sky,
Along the stream where your shade is nearby.
The sandstorm with lightning is sweeping o'er,
Other things fall while you remain high.

咏胡杨

之六十四

云乱高枝雪满川，
春生秋后复冬眠。
沉沙冷暖谁先觉？
除却胡桐不是天。

Odes to Diversifolious Poplars (No.64)

In fleeting wild cloud and stream-filling snow,
Born in spring, in other seasons you grow.
The coldness and warmth in the desert deep
'Tis you that are the first to feel and know.

咏胡杨

之六十五

阅尽沧桑古木王，

前朝之树后乘凉。

同根你我无分别，

围绕心源汇所长。

注：新疆沙雅县其乃巴格村，有一棵由数棵胡杨合抱而成的胡杨，
树围过 8 米，树龄 1500 年，人称胡杨王。

Odes to Diversifolious Poplars (No.65)

This is the weather-beaten poplar king
Which our generations its good does bring.
Its same roots other poplar' roots do share,
To the advantages all these trees cling.

Note: There is a diversifolious poplar which is 1500 years old and is 8 meters
around named the King of Diversifolious Poplars in Qinaibag Village in Shaya
County.

咏胡杨

之六十六

边陲秋在万丛巅，
与人同悟是心源。
精神一点成金色，
望到白云天那边。

Odes to Diversifolious Poplars (No.66)

The fall lights on the treetop at th' frontier,
The secret of which with men is made clear.
The spirit as such has turned into gold
Which beyond the cloud and sky one can peer.

咏胡杨

之六十七

薄暮边陲秀满堆，

隔窗但见雪纷飞。

凌风老叶声声吼，

是问春天何日回。

Odes to Diversifolious Poplars (No.67)

At dusk piles of brocade at the frontier
Are falling snowflakes out of windows here.
The old leaves in the wind are crying loud
To ask when the vernal days will appear?

咏胡杨

之六十八

自知瀚海流沙苦，
不效群芳恋岭南。
代代西陲护边老，
春风慨叹绿前川。

Odes to Diversifolious Poplars (No.68)

Knowing the hardship in the flowing sand,
You don't follow the plants in th' southern land,
Guarding th' western frontier year after year,
E'en spring breeze is moved t' offer a green hand.

咏胡杨

之六十九

塔河东去越洪荒，
流水汤汤晚带香。
内有胡杨千滴泪，
牛耕岂忍作琼浆。

Odes to Diversifolious Poplars (No.69)

River Ta runs east o'er the wasteland vast,
With the trees' fragrance of late flowing past.
How can plowing oxen drink th' water there
As it carries teardrops from such trees cast.

咏胡杨

之七十

秋来塞外起惊涛，
风压霜欺未折腰。
摧骨狂沙权当浴，
还将信念写枝条。

Odes to Diversifolious Poplars (No.70)

Stirring storms arise at th' frontier in fall,
In bullying wind and frost you never fall.
The bone-breaking storm is just bath for you,
Your faith is the most vital thing of all.

咏胡杨

之七十一

不比江南桃李妖，
荒川作伍最英豪。
情深万丈埋根底，
铁臂柔条意自娇。

Odes to Diversifolious Poplars (No.71)

Different from the southern plum and peach,
You are the heroes in the wasteland's reach.
Your great emotion is deep in your roots,
Your iron arms of boughs are graceful each.

咏胡杨

之七十二

一卧荒原百岁身，
何须儿女共沾襟。
多情红柳知音在，
不必天涯若比邻。

Odes to Diversifolious Poplars (No.72)

You spend all your life here in the wasteland,
No need to o'eruse common people's tear gland.
The lovely Chinese Tamarisk's with you,
No need to have friends from the remote land.

咏胡杨

之七十三

蒸沙铄石火云煎，
魂在荒原力在肩。
只愿天公重抖擞，
银河一泻到边关。

Odes to Diversifolious Poplars (No.73)

Stirred and steamed and burned by sand, stone and cloud,
Task burdened, your soul the wasteland does shroud.
Would that Heaven re-pour the Milky Way
To enliven here and make you fresh-boughed.

咏胡杨

之七十四

贵贱难移傲骨铮，

兴衰荣辱一毛轻。

修成孝子三千载，

铁血金身铸汗青。

Odes to Diversifolious Poplars (No.74)

Noble or humble, nothing moves your mind,
With all glories and insults left behind.
You have been filial for three thousand years,
With your warm blood and golden bones combined.

咏胡杨

之七十五

无论枝枯与叶青，
平沙杂处傍云生。
人言塞外霜来早，
猎猎天风共我鸣。

Odes to Diversifolious Poplars (No.75)

Whether verdant or withered your boughs are,
In sands you dwell close to many a star.
Frosts come early at the frontier, they say,
Where sough with you the high winds from afar.

咏胡杨

之七十六

胡杨根底白杨身，
碱海难移寒岁心。
高耸身材非自显，
秋来欲抚碧天云。

Odes to Diversifolious Poplars (No.76)

You're born of the great poplar family,
Standing firm in th' cold sea of alkali.
Your tallness is not a show of your height,
But a caress for th' clouds in the blue sky.

咏胡杨

之七十七

瀚海边陲沙气蒸，
无关翠叶起葱茏。
一生百死曾经过，
权作桑拿更放松。

Odes to Diversifolious Poplars (No.77)

The sea of sands steaming at the frontier
Does not care to make your leaves verdant here.
You've experienced countless deaths in your life,
Taking as relaxing Sauna th' heat drear.

咏胡杨

之七十八

看似空心实热心，
上天入地道行深。
惊雷伴舞阳关曲，
几朵娇花可识音？

Odes to Diversifolious Poplars (No.78)

You seem to be hollow but own a warm heart,
Deeply rooted, in th' sky remains your part.
You dance with great thunders at the frontier,
No ordinary flowers will understand your art.

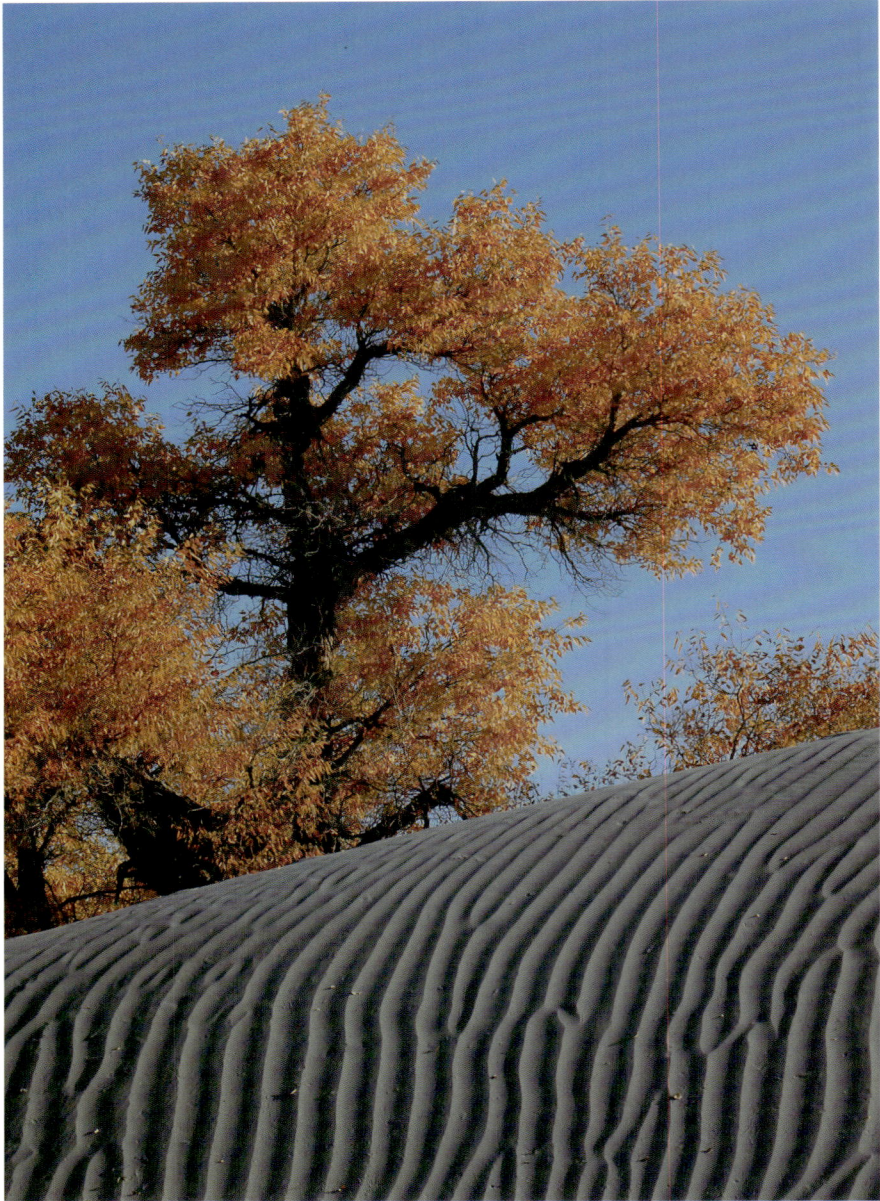

咏胡杨

之七十九

静卧寒沙秋正浓，
节操不与众芳同。
金风欲我冬眠早，
好向来年绿万重。

Odes to Diversifolious Poplars (No.79)

In deep autumn you lie over th' sand drear,
Diff'rent from others to fame you adhere.
The west wind wants you to hibernate soon,
To make a stretch of green in the next year.

咏胡杨

之八十

朔风卷雪漱寒枝，

守土苍凉我最痴。

梦里灵根忽闪亮，

未醒已得一行诗。

Odes to Diversifolious Poplars (No.80)

Washing your boughs the northern wind with snow,
You're th' most steadfast to guard the land, you know.
You have caught inspiration in your dream,
Before you wake a line of verse does show.

咏胡杨

之八十一

风舞黄云鸟不飞，
时闻绝漠吼惊雷。
分明电闪时空退，
疑是沙驼负重归。

Odes to Diversifolious Poplars (No.81)

The fleeting clouds dancing where no birds fly,
O'er the desert thunders are heard on high.
You're camel teams on your way back with loads
When lightning and thunder go back to th' sky.

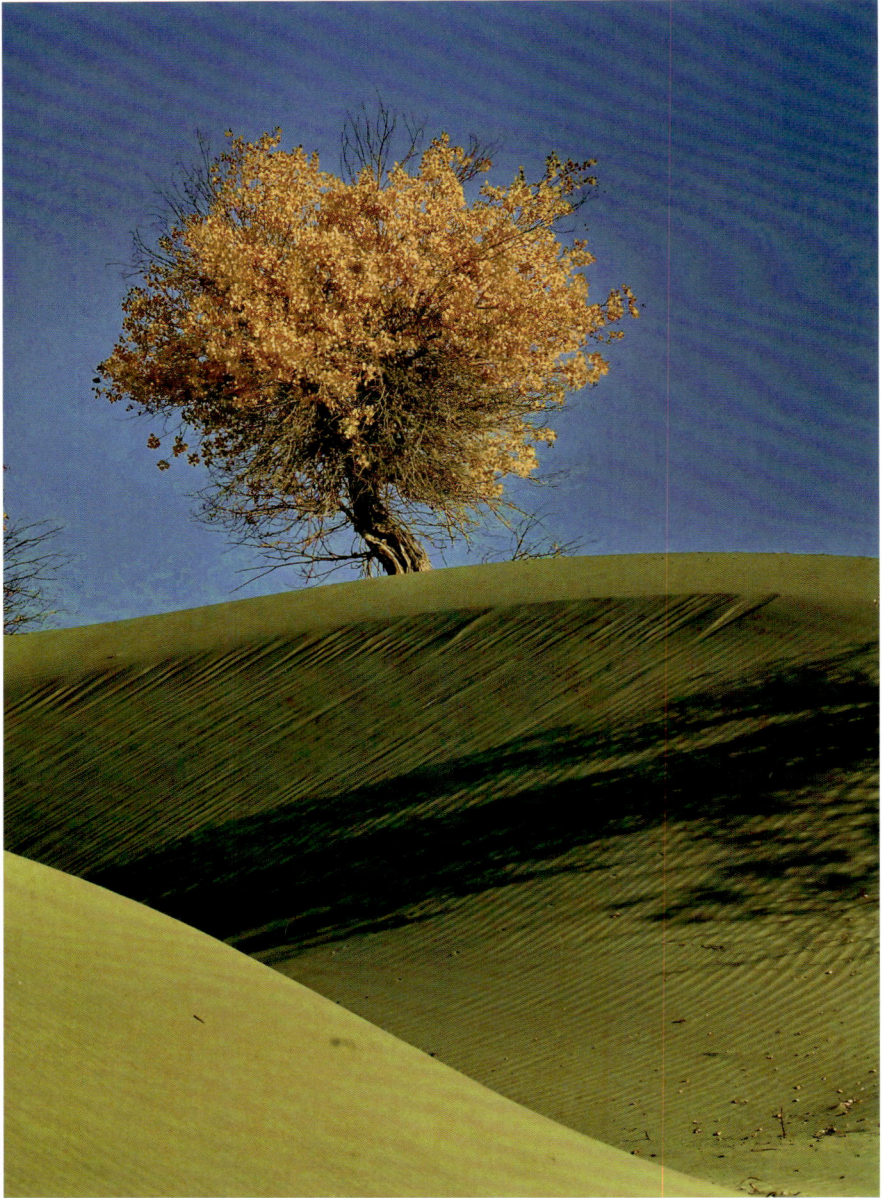

咏胡杨

之八十二

不缘地僻减精神，
纵死尤崇梁父吟。
小草离家成远志，
此身长做戍边人。

Odes to Diversifolious Poplars (No.82)

You are in high spirit though out of th' way,
Venturing to make your heroic lay.
Far away from home, you got a great goal,
At th' frontier you make an eternal stay.

咏胡杨

之八十三

傲雪凌霜伴热肠，
风光不占隐洪荒。
生前死后三千载，
总把沙原作故乡。

Odes to Diversifolious Poplars (No.83)

Deigning snow and frost with all your warm heart,
In the wasteland you play a secluded part.
You've spent your life here for three thousand years,
Regarding th' desert as your homeland smart.

咏胡杨

之八十四

英雄一别隔三年，
犹忆沙风夜月寒。
属意秋声传我意，
穿林抚叶最须怜。

注：胡杨树在新疆又被称为英雄树。

Odes to Diversifolious Poplars (No.84)

A hero's departed for three years of time,
With sand, wind, moonlight and cold as its prime.
You tell the autumn to pass what you mean,
To caress the forest-leaves in this clime.

Note: In Xinjiang, the diversifolious poplar is also named the hero tree.

咏胡杨

之八十五

风雷起处动群声，
远近高低听树鸣。
再借回天千载力，
沙荒可向绿洲行。

Odes to Diversifolious Poplars (No.85)

The ground-shaking wind and thunder arise,
Far and near, high and low, heard are trees' cries.
Would that the heavenly power of savior
Be used to green th' desert to a great size.

咏胡杨

之八十六

立身沙碛史无名，
写尽风流未有声。
莫把灵躯作痴物，
须知生死是忠诚。

Odes to Diversifolious Poplars (No.86)

In history, your life in the sands' unknown,
All your silent heroic deeds not shown.
No one should take your divine trunk as husk,
Your eternal devotion you do own.

咏胡杨

之八十七

河畔荒丘矗有年，
铜身铁臂翠黄间。
不知满眼杨花舞，
疑是初冬雪满天。

Odes to Diversifolious Poplars (No.87)

Long have you stood high along th' riverside,
Brass-bodied and iron-armed in hues wide.
Not knowing catkins dancing before eyes,
They can be snowflakes on the winter's ride.

咏胡杨

之八十八

夕阳苍眼挂平沙，
绒伞飘零处处家。
奔走匆匆沟壑满，
安求寸土发新芽？

Odes to Diversifolious Poplars (No.88)

A vast stretch of sand veiled in th' setting sun,
Where umbrella-like downs drift one by one.
To fill in ditches, they alight in haste,
To seek an inch of the sprouting place? —None!

咏胡杨

之八十九

北风卷叶去无情，
留与荒原满目清。
大雪真心来送水，
新春回报绿盈盈。

Odes to Diversifolious Poplars (No.89)

Your leaves swept away in the northern wind,
On the wasteland with bald trees left behind.
The great snow sends water out of its power,
The next spring relives with all hues combined.

咏胡杨

之九十

向风长啸慰平生，
为阻荒沙甘作屏。
大爱此番谁得晓，
影人摄去好参评。

Odes to Diversifolious Poplars (No.90)

The soughing wind there is your lifelong sigh,
As a screen the barren sand you defy.
Who can make your greatest love known this time?
The photographers hold your image high.

咏胡杨

之九十一

西风荡荡起西畴，

沙海常闻涌蜃楼。

万木霜天今日始，

听君一语已惊秋。

Odes to Diversifolious Poplars (No.91)

A sweeping wind arises from the west,
On the sand-sea is heard th' mirage to rest.
The frost comes to the trees from today on,
Th' news of which you proclaim and manifest.

咏胡杨

之九十二

西风掠地万千刀，
守土安能让一毫？
百代烟消犹似昨，
月光照我忆前朝。

Odes to Diversifolious Poplars (No.92)

Like swords, the western wind has cut the ground
Which needs to be defended safe and sound.
The smoke of battles is like yesterday,
The moonlight me recalling th' past has found.

咏胡杨

之九十三

小叶枝头半抹青，
流沙灼面已无惊。
年轮写满千秋雪，
枯干犹存八面风。

Odes to Diversifolious Poplars (No.93)

The little leaves just yellow on your boughs,
Burning your face th' flowing sand as one knows.
You remain valiant though withered and dried,
Recording the year-rings with timeless snows.

咏胡杨

之九十四

遥看如画又如云，
未上瑶台已绝尘。
信得刀风蚀筋骨，
如同郢匠铸铜身。

Odes to Diversifolious Poplars (No.94)

Just a scene or cloud from a distant view,
Your specialty makes a celestial show.
Cuts by the knife of wind deep in your bones
Make you a copper-sculpture as all know.

咏胡杨

之九十五

河水断流枯木横，
诗人到此忆伶仃。
斧下留情多爱意，
莫教空嗟墓志铭。

Odes to Diversifolious Poplars (No.95)

The riverbed dries and dead trees crisscross,
Seeing th' lonely scene th' poet feels at loss.
Please leave more of your love here, the hatchet,
Don't just have stone inscriptions in the moss.

咏胡杨

之九十六

老去犹能立大荒，
游人止步泪千行。
何当共挽胡杨臂，
万里边关筑绿廊。

Odes to Diversifolious Poplars (No.96)

In your old age you still stand in th' wasteland,
In tears the travelers stop at the scene grand.
How we wish to embrace your poplar's arms,
So that the long frontier's armed with green band.

咏胡杨

之九十七

七月流火到天涯，

望断荒原何处家。

我劝行云多驻足，

长将甘雨沃龙沙。

Odes to Diversifolious Poplars (No.97)

In the seventh moon's heat here you have come,

On the remote wasteland far from your home.

I ask the fleeting cloud to stop here more,

And send to the sands its sweet rain as foam.

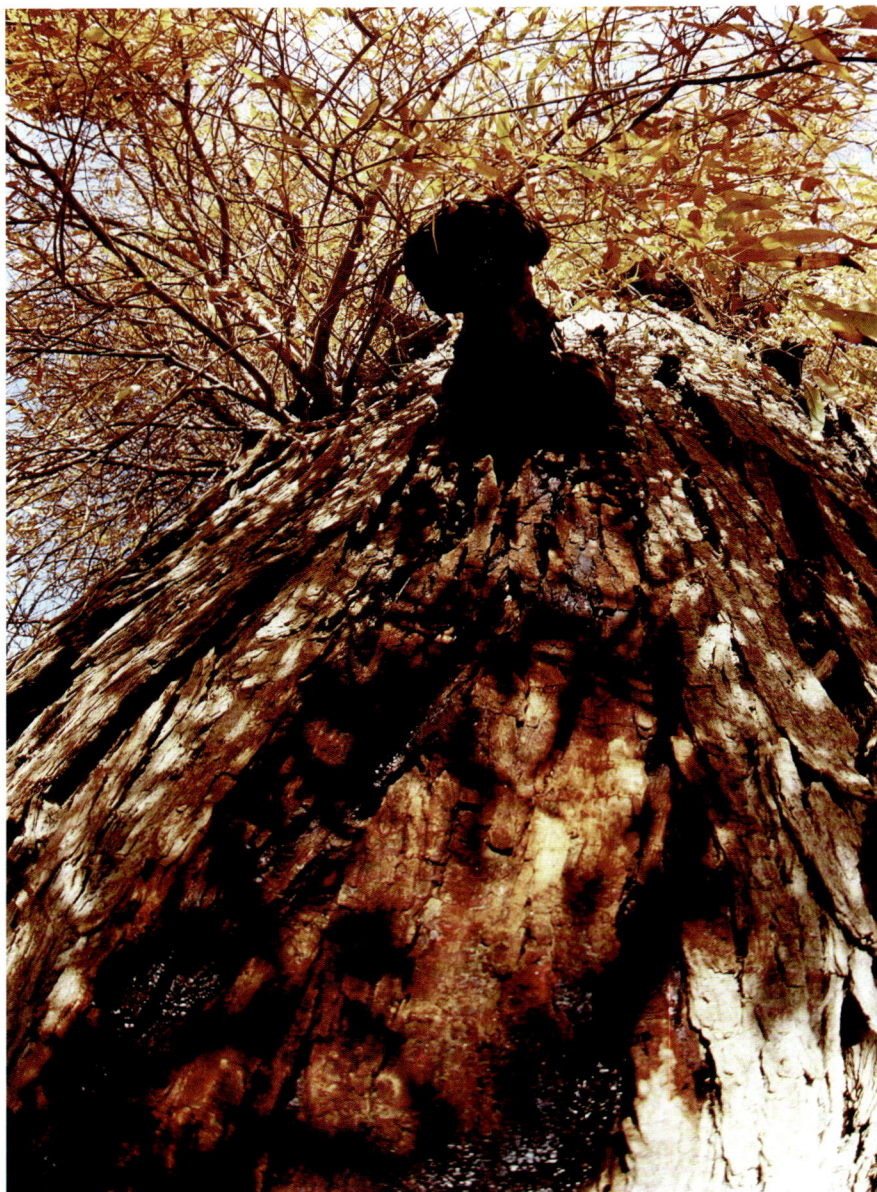

咏胡杨

之九十八

窗外胡杨扑面来，
苍颜未老叶先衰。
多情我欲长相守，
化作芦花脚下开。

Odes to Diversifolious Poplars (No.98)

Outside th' train window poplars meet my eyes,
Your leaves wither before your black trunk dies.
I would like to stay with you for years long,
And turn to be reed that at your foot lies.

咏胡杨

之九十九

独立沙原几度秋，
苍凉已改少年头。
长将巨痛埋心底，
不遇知音不泪流。

Odes to Diversifolious Poplars (No.99)

Standing aloft over the sands for years,
Some white hair on your once young head appears.
Buried deep in your heart is your great pain,
Seeing your bosom friend you break into tears.

咏胡杨

之一〇〇

壮士黑城化此身，

秋风每度总惊魂。

而今荒野无人识，

却笑西天有怪神。

注：怪树林，传说将士黑城突围后在这里全部战死，躯体变成了
这片胡杨林。

Odes to Diversifolious Poplars (No.100)

Th' heroes from Heicheng turned into these trees,
The western wind cannot make you at ease.
Now they know not you here in the wasteland,
And take you as strange in th' west as they please.

Note: The strange forest: Legend has it that the officers and their men were all
killed here after they broke through Heicheng (the Dark City). Their bodies
turned into this forest of diversifolious poplars.

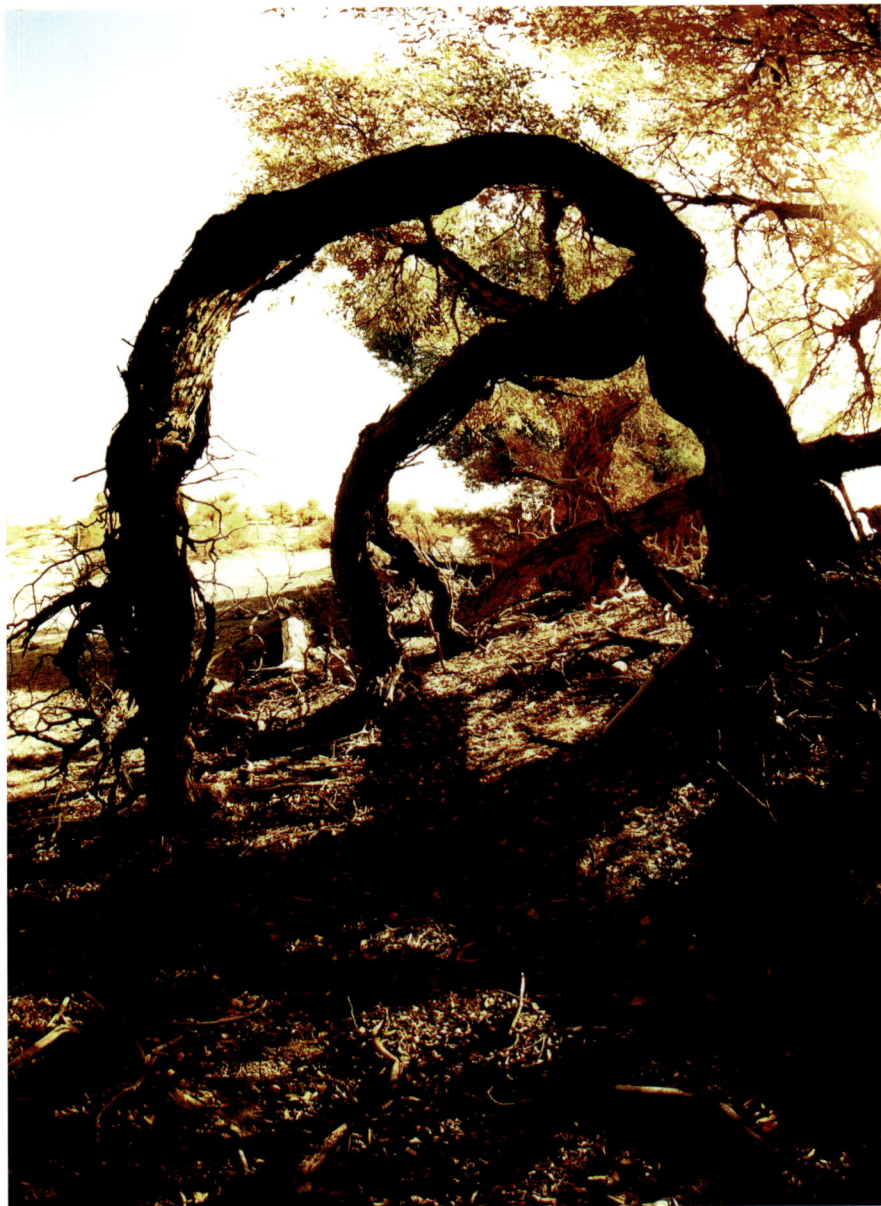

咏胡杨

之一〇一

误传三叶守基因，
躯干中空朽木身。
不解南疆河畔树，
高枝同样可凌云。

注：有的胡杨一棵树上有三种形状的叶子，因此胡杨又被称为三叶树。

Odes to Diversifolious Poplars (No.101)

Your three types of leaves are rumored t' keep gene,
Hollow-trunked, your decayed body is seen.
The riverside trees at th' southern frontier
Have been as high as fleeting clouds have been.

Note: Some of the diversifolious poplars have three types of leaves and therefore renamed three-type-of-leaf tree.

咏胡杨

之一〇二

情字煌煌何以论，
荒原大隐有封神。
青春老去终无悔，
立地能为佛一尊。

Odes to Diversifolious Poplars (No.102)

Love is not enough to show your heart fair,
Canonized on th' wasteland is your part rare.
You ne'er regret your youth spent in th' wasteland,
Standing as a grand statue of Buddha there.

咏胡杨

之一〇三

千年沙海自风光，
盘古开天一画堂。
我在黄沙堆里卧，
于诗于画补沧桑。

Odes to Diversifolious Poplars (No.103)

A thousand years of sand-sea's a grand view,
Since th' beginning of th' world, it's the first show.
You lie in piles and piles of yellow sands,
Th' pastoral and pictorial scenes t' renew.

咏胡杨

之一〇四

沧桑百代雾茫茫，
感慨迢迢向远方。
最怕残阳慢慢落，
眼前如洒血行行。

Odes to Diversifolious Poplars (No.104)

Throughout the ages changes in fog-veil,
Into a farther place you further trail.
You fear the slow, slow setting of the sun,
Just like a spread of blood on a large scale.

咏胡杨

之一〇五

边陲谁道无风景，
万里黄沙万里金。
一望长天慷慨甚，
有云片片报春心。

Odes to Diversifolious Poplars (No.105)

Who says there's no scene at th' frontier?
Ten thousand miles of sands are golden here.
The boundless sky is a generous view
Where clouds are the rewards which are paid dear.

咏 胡 杨

之一〇六

片片高天片片情，
曾经携手岸边行。
忍看战友凌风倒，
再展云梢月下横。

Odes to Diversifolious Poplars (No.106)

Your boundless passion fills the boundless sky,
Walking along th' bank with comrades nearby.
Seeing your comrades falling in the wind,
Into the moon you extend your boughs high.

咏胡杨

之一○七

寂寂沙原日影斜，

云边极目似天涯。

胡笳曲曲沙洲泪，

阅尽沧桑随处家。

Odes to Diversifolious Poplars (No.107)

The sun slanting over the silent sands,
A stretch of clouds is where your eye expands.
The pipes played herein provoke your tears here,
The changes of th' world are all your homelands.

肖路凡 摄

咏胡杨

之一〇八

此身不叹沧州老，

长戍天山乐五更。

生死何须关内外，

千年本色尚忠诚。

注：陆游词《诉衷情》以"此身谁料，心在天山，身老沧州"表
达现实境遇与胸怀大志的矛盾。此处反其意而用之。

Odes to Diversifolious Poplars (No.108)

You ne'er regret getting old in Cangzhou,
You e'en enjoy safeguarding Tianshan, though.
Spending your life anywhere at the pass,
An eternal heart of devotion you grow.

Note: Lu You expressed his great ideal in contrast with the reality in his ci-poem entitled "Suzhongqing" which says, "Who can expect that/ my goal aims at Tianshan/ While I grow old at Cangzhou". Here in the ode is a contrary use of the lines.

咏胡杨

之一〇九

驼风古道影憧憧，
夜枕沙丘梦大风。
漠北天生多奇士，
林林百万似虬龙。

Odes to Diversifolious Poplars (No.109)

On distant ancient paths loom camels' band,
Safeguarding th' frontier is your dream on th' sand.
Valiant trees are born to live in th' northwest,
In multitude, you're dragons powerful and grand.

王瀚林《胡杨百咏》译后记

杨　虚

　　去年夏，接到新疆生产建设兵团王瀚林先生的邮件和电话，嘱译其《胡杨百咏》。由于工作繁忙，此前对军旅诗歌和诗人王瀚林先生并不熟悉，只是在唐诗宋词中读到边塞诗，如王昌龄的《出塞》、王维的《使至塞上》、岑参的《走马川行奉送封大夫出师西征》、范仲淹的《渔家傲·塞下秋来风景异》等，其特有的风格给我留下了深刻的印象。拜读了瀚林先生的《胡杨百咏》后，感到这样专咏胡杨的边塞诗和军旅诗，一写就是一百余首，诗歌史上少见，在当今社会更为难得。

　　《胡杨百咏》是吟咏新疆胡杨的组诗，采用七绝的诗体来表现，既继承了传统格律诗歌创作中的边塞诗特有的豪放风格，又在当今诗歌创作和社会风气中不为庸俗的时风所动，别有风情地歌颂了军人乐于奉献的高贵精神和军旅生活的豪情壮志。在当下的诗歌写作中发扬了传统，弘扬了正气，开启了后人，可谓独树一帜。

　　一百余首的七绝组诗中，诗人所表现的思想是丰富的，既有胡杨的侠骨，又有胡杨的柔肠。如第二十七首："老去犹能立大荒，不知此地是他乡。擎天一帜寒沙上，还为游人作导航"；第二十八首："黑沙尘骤起孤烟，宛若苍龙舞破原。劫尽精华筋骨在，高枝剑指九重天"，"擎天一帜"、"剑指九天"，表现侠骨，十分独到地写出了胡杨的"军人"特质。第十六首："轻风抚面对妆台，含笑君从镜底来。十里金黄何所似？任人想象任人猜"；第四十七首："多情看似恰无情，深隐荒原情最深。老去无名终不悔，立身塞外舞清音"，"轻风抚面"、"身舞清音"，写柔肠，也道出了胡杨的特殊美姿。诗人在胡杨意象的表达上颇有独特之处，如"铮铮铁骨弄风华，宛若苍龙戏晚霞"（第六十首），像这样遒劲而壮美的诗句，在《胡杨百咏》中还有很多，恕不一一枚举。全组诗就是我们戍边将士生活感情的写照，诗人从各个方面歌颂了胡杨的形象，写的就是他们甜酸苦辣军旅之情，就是他们的爱恨情仇。这是军人的诗，是"马背"上的诗，是别的诗人不可代替的诗！诗人旧诗功底深厚，用语娴熟，表现力强，很多句式和表现手法都脱胎于文学史上的著名诗行，如"狂飙漫卷龙沙起，送我诗情到碧霄"（第五首），就是化用了刘禹锡的"晴空一鹤排云上，便引诗情到碧霄"（《秋词》）；又如"枯卧荒原不自悲，长思奋力洒芳菲"（第六十二首），化用了陆游的"僵卧孤村不自哀，尚思为国戍轮台"（《十一月四日风雨大作》）。如此等等，不一而足。与此同时，他全组诗的主题表现了强烈的时代气息，提倡了甘于奉献的精神，力图挽救诗坛的颓风。在当今一片铜臭的社会风气中，瀚林的这些军旅作品给我们吹来了一股清风，让我们心灵净化，让我们思想脱俗，知道这个社会还是有崇高，还是有伟大。

我是在心灵受到洗礼的同时投入感情进行这些诗歌作品英译的。对"百咏"诗题，我采用了英文的 ode to（……颂歌）一词，而未采用 verse on（……咏），这符合英诗诗题传统，也从更深的层次理解瀚林先生"百咏"的精神。此外，对瀚林先生七绝的格律和押韵方式，我采用了英诗的五步抑扬格和 aaba 的韵式，大体上和原作有对应的关系。在选词造句上，我尽量注重英译的流畅性和诗意的深度，表现原诗的神韵，而不逐字照译。如第二十一首："盘根千载意何求？唯愿边畴尽绿洲。岂与群芳争俏丽，寸心热血写风流。"我将其英译为："Your aim of age-old intricate roots' net / Is to make oases in the border set / Rather than vie beauty with other flowers / So that special grace you strive for and get."（Odes to Diversifolious Poplars, No.21）这里，我的英译充分使用了英诗语言的特色，全诗是一个句子，每行的格律和韵脚都是自然的语句顺序安排，原文的诗意化在其中。在此稍作分析："盘根"译作 intricate roots' net，net 为增译，补足语义，也为后文"尽绿洲"作伏笔，当然该词的选用还为了押韵；"千载"译作 age-old，作定语使用；"意何求"的疑问语气，英译中转换成陈述的语气，这样就能让英文连缀成一个句子，因此处理成了 your aim...is...；从原文诗意上看，"意何求"与"唯愿"是一问一答的行文方式，实乃一意，故有上译，"唯愿"的心意在英诗中还通过动词不定式短语 to make...set 加以补足；"边畴"译为 the border，即边塞之意，原文的"边畴"亦为"边塞"义，是因为平仄的原因调成"边畴"的；"尽绿洲"译作英文复数的 oases，表示数目多，这是发挥了英诗中语法概念的作用；原文第三句是个反问句，意即"不与群芳争俏丽"，故此，英译成了 rather than vie beauty with other flowers，正好构成英诗的一个完整句子；末句的英译处理为表示结果或目的的从属句；这里的"写"与前句的"争"是一个意思，同时也兼含"成就"义，故英译为 So that special grace you strive for and get；"风流"一词是汉诗中的传统用法，含有"风流人物"、"时代风流"之意，英译使用了 special grace，强调了胡杨的体姿和意态之美。原作咏胡杨主要使用了第一人称，或第三人称，我在英译中依照雪莱《西风颂》等英诗的习惯，统一使用了第二人称，表现了诗人是用对话的语气称颂胡杨，同时强调了拟人的手法，这是为了生动表达的需要而作的相应变化。

英译工作终于完成了，回头看看，又是一个夏天，过去了一年的光景。瀚林先生在中间给我打过一次电话，询问进展情况。答应先生英译，又因时序如流，工作繁多，影响了进度，对先生怀有歉意。现在对着这些英译的文本，总算舒了口气，完成了先生的嘱托，英译本虽然算不上上乘，但也做到了严守英诗格律，行文流畅，基本把握了原作的灵魂。他日如有机会见面，也可谈谈英译时的感受，和因英译而结下的特有诗谊，却也应着李商隐的《雨夜寄北》："何当共剪西窗烛，却话巴山夜雨时。"

2013 年 6 月 18 日
于宁波大学文萃新村竹云轩

| Postscript by Yang Xu |

Last summer, I received an email together with a telephone from Mr. Wang Hanlin in Xinjiang Production and Construction Corps, asking me to translate his *Odes to Diversifolious Poplars*. As I have been busy with my work, I did not familiarize myself with military poetry and Mr. Wang Hanlin the poet. What I knew in this field was only the border poems in Tang and Song dynasties, such as Wang Changling's "On the Frontier", Wang Wei's "An Envoy to the Frontier", Cen Shen's "Song of Running-Horse River in Farewell to General Feng on His Western Expedition" and Fan Zhongyan's "An Estranged Scene at the Border in Autumn in tune of Fishermen Proud", etc. All those verses have left me a deep impression in terms of their special style. After reading Mr. Wang Hanlin's works in question, I come to realize that such odes on one topic, more than 100 in number, are really rare and valuable in the history of poetry and our contemporary society.

Hanlin's *Odes to Diversifolious Poplars* is a set of quatrains on a special kind of tree in Xinjiang, which is both a continuation of the heroic style of the traditional border poetry and a eulogy of the contemporary soldiers' devotion, nobility and heroism, a special gem in our contemporary society and literary world. These quatrains are prominent in that they give an expression to classical poetic creation, social justice and encouragement to readers. The poet created a wealth of thought and image in these over 100 quatrains on diversifolious poplars which, under his pen, are both heroic and gentle. Examples are: "In your old age, in th' desert you still stand, / Not knowing that 'tis not your own homeland./Serving as a guide for the travelers there, /You are just a banner o'er the cold sand."(No.27) "A curl of smoke arises from dark sand, /Like wildly dancing dragon black and grand./Your bones remain though you died in kalpas, /With your skyward bough like a fighting hand."(No.28) "A banner o'er the cold sand" and "a skyward fighting hand" are heroic expressions of the "military" tree. "At the dressing table breeze strokes your face,/You come from the mirror with smiling grace./What does it look like, the ten miles of gold?/In imagination, th' scene one can trace."(No.16) "Your deep emotion seems quite a stone-heart,/In th' desert you play a secluded part./You ne'er regret getting old and obscure,/Living at th' frontier being your best art."(No.47) "Breeze strokes your face", "deep emotion as your best art" are gentle expressions of the "graceful" tree. The poet is special in his versification, the sublime lines like "Your iron of bones displays your look proud,/As if you're a dragon in th' rosy cloud" (No.60) are common in his works. The whole set of quatrains is a reflection of the emotional life of our border guards. The poet eulogizes the image of the tree from different angles in connection with the bitter and sweet military as well as emotional life. They are poems of a soldier, writing on "horseback", irreplaceable by others. The poet has a solid foundation in classical Chinese poetry, expressive in image creation and apt at wording. Many lines originate from the noted poems in the history of Chinese classical poetry. For example, "While th' golden tide of golden boughs and leaves,/Makes my sky-reaching poetic heart proud"(No.5) has its source from the Tang poet Liu Yuxi's "A Song of Autumn" which reads "A crane is flying up to clouds on high/ Drawing my poetic heart to th' azure sky." "O'er the barren land never feeling sad,/You endeavor to spread the green you've had" (No.62) has its source in the Song poet Lu You's "A Great Storm on the Fourth Day of the Eleventh Moon" which reads "Ne'er feeling sad lying in the lonely cottage here, / I am still thinking of guarding our state's frontier." Besides, his quatrains are imposing in their contemporarily right theme, emphasizing the spirit of dedication in a profiteering society. His military works of art have brought us a freshening breeze, purifying our souls, rectifying our conventional ideas, informing us of what sublimity and grandeur mean.

I went to passionately translate these works with a purified heart. I selected the term "ode to" instead of "verse on" to render the title, which, I believe, is a deeper understanding of the title. In the meantime, I used iambic pentameter and aaba rhyming scheme to imitate the original form of the Chinese seven-character quatrain. In wording, I tried my best to freely express the depth of the original instead of word-for-word or line-for-line translation. For example, the original Chinese quatrain (No. 21) has four lines which are understood as four sentences which reads "Pan gen qian zai yi he qiu? Wei yuan bianchou jin lvzhou. Qi yu qun fang zheng qiaoli, cunxin rexue xie fengliu."For a good English reading, I used one sentence to translate it: "Your aim of age-old intricate roots' net / Is to make oases in the border set / Rather than vie beauty with other flowers / So that special grace you strive for and get." Here, I took advantage of the English versification in which there was a natural arrangement of meters and rhymes while the original meaning was kept. A specific analysis is made here: "Pan gen" (coiling roots) was translated as "intricate roots' net", "net" was added for emphasis which corresponds with "to make oases". Besides that, the word was also used for rhyming. "Qian zai" (thousand years) was translated as "age-old" used as an attributive. "Yi he qiu" (for what intention) was a question, which was translated into a statement ("your aim...is...") so that the English version sounds natural. In the original, "yi he qiu" and "wei yuan"(only wish) were in a dialogue form, and here I combined them into one sentence. The meaning of "wei yuan" was completed by an infinitive phrase "to make...set". "Bianchou" (border and field) was simplified as "the border". "Jin lvzhou"(all oases) was translated into "oases" a plural form, whereas the English grammatical notion was applied. The third line in the original is a rhetorical question, which, then, was translated as "rather than vie beauty with other flowers" so that a natural English sentence was formed. The last line in the original was changed into a subordinate clause of result or purpose. The "xie" (write) here means the same with "zheng" (vie) in the former line, both meaning "achieving". Therefore, it was translated as "so that special grace you strive for and get." Here, "special grace" was used to render "fengliu" which means both "fashionable celebrities" and "fashion of the time". By such a phrase, I emphasized the physical and stylistic beauty of the tree. The poet used the first person or the third person to eulogize the tree. In the English version, I used the second person as Shelley did in his "Ode to the West Wind". By using the second person, I personified the tree so that its image is better combined with the spirit of our soldiers.

Finally I completed my task which has taken me a whole year. Hanlin telephoned me once during my task to ask for the progress of translation. I felt sorry for him as I delayed the work for the swift passage of time and my own teaching and research work. And now I feel somewhat relieved with the completion of the task. I have done what was asked and basically I have done a satisfactory job though my English version is not among the best. I stick to the meters and fluency of the version while I have kept the original meaning. If we have got any chance to meet someday, I may tell Hanlin how I felt in translation. With such a task, I have made friends with a soldier-poet to my honor. The Tang poet Li Shanyin's lines of "when by our window can we trim the wicks again/ And talk about this endless dreary night of rain ("To the North in a Rainy Night", tr. X.Y.Z.)" can express what I am feeling now.

Zhunyunxuan, Wencui Xincun, Ningbo University,

June 18, 2013

《胡杨百咏》后记

在边疆生活工作久了，经常被一些人和事感动。每次来到孙龙珍纪念馆，看到烈士生前为未出生的孩子缝制的衣服，就会想到孙龙珍为营救被敌人掳去的职工，身怀六甲的她手持铁锹冲向敌人，倒在弹雨中，腹中胎儿还在她温热犹存的体内蠕动的惨烈场面。每次来到军垦新城石河子看到军垦每一楼，都会想到当年战士们在零下四十度气温下，从几十公里外用爬犁运木材，滴水成冰，哈气成霜，小伙子们浑身挂满天鹅绒般的白色茸毛，个个变成了白须白眉白头发的"小寿星"的感人场景。每次在边境线上看到那些以种地为站岗、以放牧为巡逻的可敬的军垦人，听到他们尽情唱着"面对蜿蜒的界河，背靠伟大的祖国。我们种地就是站岗，我们放牧就是巡逻。要问军垦战士想的是什么？祖国的繁荣昌盛就是我最大的欢乐……"的时候，我心里总是被感动着，总想把这些感人的事情记录下来。

有一次中央领导同志来新疆视察，提到要学习大漠胡杨、戈壁红柳、天山雪松和绿洲白杨的精神，我的心弦被拨动了。这几种植物在新疆都是常见的，它们与军垦精神之间真的有种天人合一的内在一致性，特别是胡杨，让我感动最深，于是萌发了借胡杨歌咏军垦精神的念头。有了这个想法，就开始构思，在出差的飞机上、宾馆里，在调研途中的汽车上，满脑子都是胡杨的影子，就这样几天一首，一天几首，几个月下来居然写了一百多首。这些诗在兵团日报刊出后，诗友们提议将其结集出版。一个偶然的机会看到杨成虎教授的译作，极有水准。诗友建议请杨先生将胡杨诗译成英文，以便传播更广。我与杨先生并不相识，但还是冒昧拨通了先生电话，杨先生教学科研任务十分繁重，但还是欣然应允，并很快就提交了高水平的译文，这让我十分钦佩和感动。

《胡杨百咏》是个宠儿，她的问世得到了大家的关心和支持，不少人为之付出了辛劳。感谢著名学者、诗人、翻译家杨成虎教授，他传神的英译让更多的人能够感悟胡杨精神的精髓；感谢中华诗词学会常务副会长李文朝将军，他的序深化了人们对胡杨精神与戍边军人精神的内在联系的理解；感谢著名作家、诗人张伯元先生，他对诗歌提出了多处修改意见；感谢沈鹏、戴本颢等著名书法家，感谢廖周炎、谷水清等摄影家，他们的作品为本书添彩不少；感谢中华文学基金会，他们独具慧眼，资助本书的出版；感谢东方出版社的同志们，他们为本书的出版付出了辛苦努力。没有大家合作，就不会有本书的问世。

王瀚林

2013 年 8 月 21 日

| Postscript by Wang Hanlin |

I have been frequently moved by the people and the events since I began to live in Xinjiang, China. Every time I visit Sun Longzhen Memorial Room, I am stirred by the clothes she made for her unborn kid which reminds me of the scenes when in order to rescue the employees captured by the enemy, she, in pregnancy, dashed towards them with a spade and fell in the rain of bullets and the feotus was alive in her still warm belly. Every time I come to Shihezi, the new military farmland, I seem to see in each building the soldiers in the old days transporting lumbers on sleighs from dozens of kilometers away under the temperature of 40 ℃ below zero when all water was frozen and their breathing air frosted. The young soldiers became downy and "white-haired old men". Every time I arrive at the border line, I see those beloved farming soldiers who guard while farming and patrol while herding. They are heard to sing "Facing the winding border stream, against our great motherland I lean. We farm our land to guard; we herd our cattle to patrol. If you ask me who our hearts measure? A flourishing motherland is my best pleasure." I 'm inclined to record all these moving scenes.

Once, a leading comrade of the central authorities came to inspect Xinjiang, and he mentioned that we need to learn from the diversifolious poplar in the sands, the tamarisk in the Gobi desert, the cedar in the Tianshan Mountains, the poplar in the oases, I was much inspired by it. These plants are common in Xinjiang which correspond with the spirit of our military farming, and the diversifolious poplar is a special example. Then, I came to the idea that I eulogize the military farming in terms of the tree in question. I began to conceive lines on the diversifolious poplar. Whether on the plane, or in the bus, I was occupied with the image of such kind of tree on my errand. Sometimes, I wrote several quatrains a day and wrote a quatrain several days and the quatrains amounted to over 100 in several months of time. When they were published on the Corps Daily, my poet-friends proposed that I publish them in a collected form. I came upon Prof. Yang Chenghu's translation of poems which were of high quality. My friends suggested that I ask him to translate my quatrains into English so that they could be read by more readers. I did not meet Prof. Yang at any occasion, but I ventured to give him a telephone call and he agreed to take the task though he was pretty busy with his work of teaching and research. After some time, he offered me his good translated versions, which moved me much.

Odes to Diversifolious Poplars is a pet, whose birth is due to many people's effort, caress and support. Here special thanks go to Prof. Yang Chenghu (Yang Xu), a scholar, poet and translator whose English versions of the quatrains enable more people to understand the spirit of diversifolious poplars, to General Li Wenchao, a standing vice president of Chinese Poetry Society whose preface deepens the understanding of the image of the tree and the spirit of our border guards, to Mr. Zhang Boyuan, a poet and writer who made many revisions to my work, to calligraphers Mr. Shen Peng and Mr. Dai Benhao, and photographers Mr. Liao Zhouyan and Mr. Gu Shuiqing whose works of art have brightened my book, to Chinese Literature Foundation which much valued this book and provided the money for its publication, and to the editors of Dongfang Press who made much effort to publish it. This book would not come into being without their help.

Wang Hanlin

August 21, 2013

责任编辑:卓　然
装帧设计:肖　辉

图书在版编目(CIP)数据

胡杨百咏:英汉对照/王瀚林 著;杨虚 译. -北京:东方出版社,2014.6
ISBN 978 - 7 - 5060 - 7083 - 6

Ⅰ.①胡…　Ⅱ.①王…②杨…　Ⅲ.①七言绝句-诗集-中国-当代-英、汉
Ⅳ.①I227.7

中国版本图书馆 CIP 数据核字(2013)第 295955 号

胡杨百咏

HUYANG BAIYONG

(英汉对照)

王瀚林 著　杨 虚 译

东方出版社 出版发行
(100706　北京朝阳门内大街 166 号)

北京华联印刷有限公司印刷　新华书店经销

2014 年 6 月第 1 版　2014 年 6 月北京第 1 次印刷
开本:787 毫米×1092 毫米 1/16　印张:16
字数:260 千字

ISBN 978 - 7 - 5060 - 7083 - 6　定价:66.00 元

邮购地址 100706　北京朝阳门内大街 166 号
人民东方图书销售中心　电话 (010)65250042　65289539

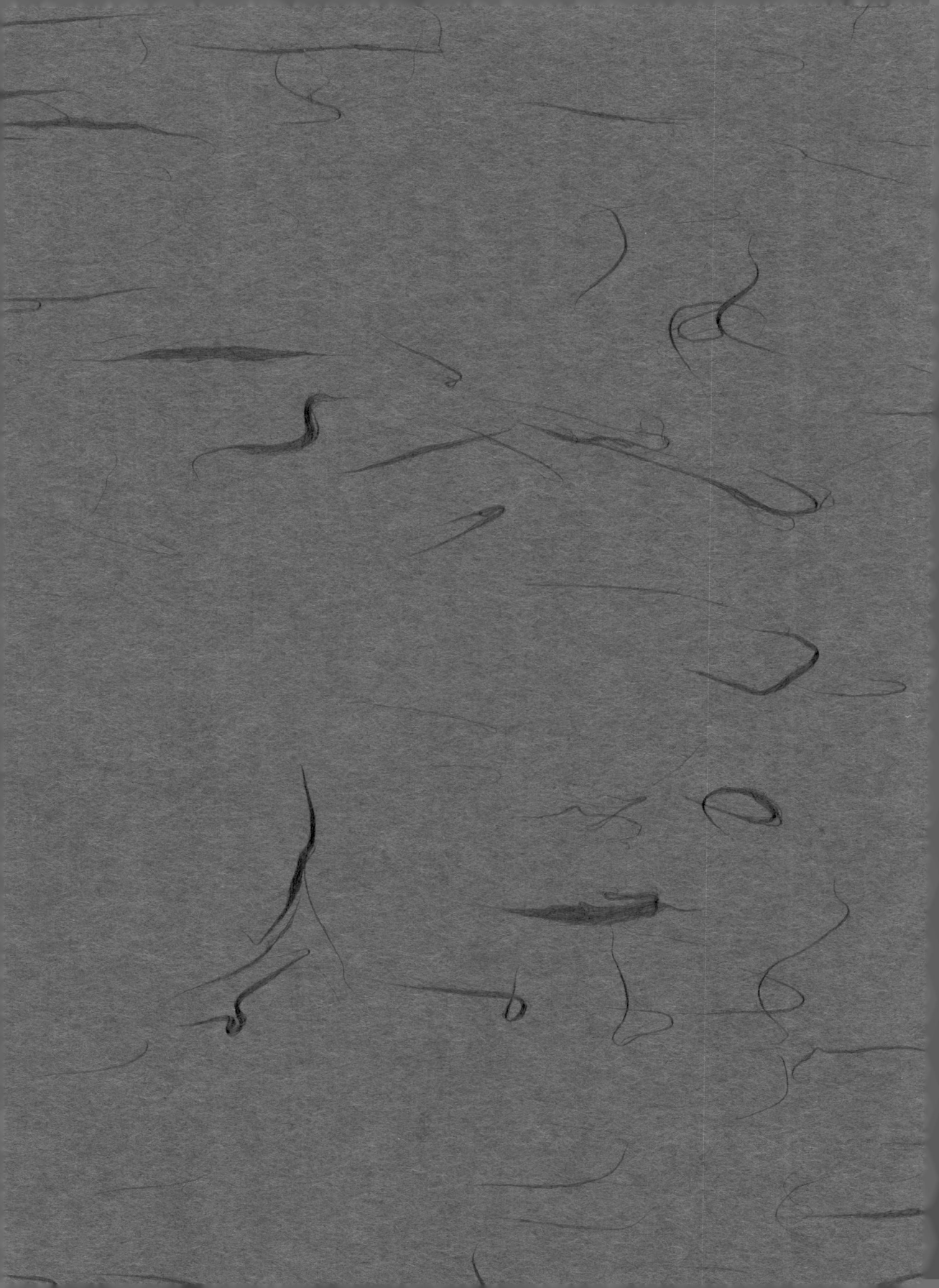